A HAUNTED HISTORY OF
COLUMBUS, OHIO

A HAUNTED HISTORY OF COLUMBUS, OHIO

NELLIE KAMPMANN

Haunted America

Published by Haunted America
A Division of The History Press
Charleston, SC 29403
www.historypress.net

First published 2011

Manufactured in the United States

ISBN 978.1.60949.087.4

Library of Congress Cataloging-in-Publication Data
Kampmann, Nellie.
A haunted history of Columbus, Ohio / Nellie Kampmann.
p. cm.
Includes bibliographical references (p.) and index.
ISBN 978-1-60949-087-4
1. Ghosts--Ohio--Columbus. 2. Columbus (Ohio)--History--Miscellanea. I. Title.
BF1472.U6K365 2011
133.109771'57--dc22
2011014952

Notice: The information in this book is true and complete to the best of our knowledge. It is offered without guarantee on the part of the author or The History Press. The author and The History Press disclaim all liability in connection with the use of this book.

The boundaries which divide Life from Death are at best shadowy and vague.
Who shall say where the one ends, and where the other begins?
—Edgar Allan Poe

CONTENTS

Preface 9
Acknowledgements 13
Introduction 15

1. Forgotten Souls: Franklin County Poor House 23
2. School Spirits: The Ohio State University 29
3. The House of Secrets: Kelton House Museum and Garden 34
4. The Ghost Who Wasn't: Westerville 42
5. Political Haunts: The Snowden-Gray House 48
6. Phantoms of War: Franklinton 52
7. Booze and Spirits: The Jury Room 57
8. On the River's Edge: Dublin 62
9. The Souls of Hospitality: Harrison House Bed & Breakfast 66
10. Murder, Mayhem and Manifestations: The Ohio State University Neighborhoods 73
11. Stage Fright: Palace Theatre 77
12. Ghosts in Masquerade: Kampmann Costume Company 82
13. The Dapper Spirit: Franklin Avenue 87
14. The River of Death: Franklinton 90
15. Quiet Souls: The Ohio State University Main Library 94
16. When the Lights Go Out: Ohio Theatre 102

Bibliography and References 109
About the Author 112

PREFACE

On a pleasant April day, three docents from the Kelton House Museum and Garden were walking back down East Town Street from the Ohio Statehouse. As befitting the event they had just attended, a reenactment of mourning for President Lincoln, they were dressed in black Civil War–era mourning gowns. A tourist who had been taking pictures of the lovely Victorian houses on the street caught sight of them and did a double take. As they came near, she stopped them to talk. She looked at them wide eyed and said, "I have to ask—are you ghosts?"

It's no wonder that she might have thought that. After all, Columbus is a wildly haunted city.

Even before I had ever considered writing a book on the subject, I sat down and started making a list of known hauntings here. A ten-block area within the Discovery District alone has an average of one haunting per block. Within ten minutes, I had thought of over fifty sites within the inner belt and slightly beyond it. That didn't even include the surrounding suburbs. Then once I started writing the book, people started telling me of more and more places that had ghostly activity.

My own introduction to the stories of hauntings in Columbus came when I was five years old. A lady who worked for my father told me about her haunted bathroom where the toilet would flush by itself. A couple of years later on a school field trip to the Columbus Zoo, I was told about the now largely forgotten legend of Leatherlips, which is possibly the oldest haunting in the area. Over the years, I had many potentially ghostly experiences myself.

They were things I couldn't explain away but none quite so compelling that I would attribute them to anything otherworldly. Then I started working in a haunted building. After several years of having my clothing tugged by unseen hands, hearing voices and footsteps when no one was around—and even seeing people who weren't physically there—I am a believer.

But why would the Columbus area be so haunted? Unlike many of the other ghostly hot spots in the world, we have been free of wars and have only had comparatively small disasters. In analyzing haunted areas in general, researchers have noticed that certain physical properties are associated with the more haunted cities. These are large amounts of water and limestone or granite in the area. Columbus is short on neither. The convergence of the Scioto and Olentangy Rivers provides the former. For that matter, Spring Street was built over a natural stream, the water of which theoretically still flows beneath our city. Columbus likewise sits atop a large limestone deposit. With these natural features, Columbus is well poised to be spook central.

It also seems that the dead want their tales to be told. While I've been writing this book, I can't tell you how many times information on a haunting coincidentally popped up in the course of my daily life. Some dramatic and sad pieces of history have come to light because of this, after having been buried for generations in dusty tomes.

The freakiest coincidences involve Anna Marie Hahn, a serial killer for profit who was the first woman in Ohio to be executed by electric chair. Although she was from Cincinnati, she is buried in Columbus at the Mount Calvary Cemetery. Not long after some friends of mine and I had a discussion about the electric chair, a photograph of her mysteriously showed up on a wall that I pass by frequently. I assumed that it was a prank being played by one of my friends, but none of them would own up to it. A few days later, I was doing some microfilm newspaper research on an unrelated topic. I randomly stopped the roll of microfilm to see what page in the newspaper I was on to determine how much farther I needed to go. There, on the page I happened to stop at, was another photograph of Anna Marie Hahn. That was peculiar, but I could still pass it off as coincidence. However, the following day, I was doing online newspaper research on a different topic. Granted, this did delve into the Ohio Penitentiary but did not have anything to do with Ms. Hahn. I entered my search terms and clicked on the first article that came up. That page featured a big photograph of Anna Marie Hahn's son and an article about her execution. That was getting to be a little too coincidental for my taste. I modified the search terms and tried again. I'll be darned if the next article I clicked on didn't also prominently mention her. It was strange that she seemed to want my attention so badly. Before that, I had no thoughts of including her in this book. There were no ghost stories about her as far as I knew. I guess there are now.

A more amusing attempt to get my attention happened at the very haunted Kelton House Museum and Garden. I was there for a meeting one night. The head of the meeting had brought a bottle of champagne to celebrate some accomplishment. One of the committee members was running late, so we held off on starting the meeting until she arrived. Not one to waste an opportunity, I got out my trusty recorder and began to interview one of the ladies there about a haunting that took place in her childhood home. All of the sudden the bottle of champagne blew its cork, although not a drop of the champagne itself spilled. Since we are so used to the antics of the spirits there, we all burst out laughing. I do believe that was the spirits' way of saying, "What are we, chopped liver?"

So, here are their tales. While the dead want their tales told, those among the living aren't always keen on that. Many of the names of the living, especially in regard to private residences, have been changed to protect their privacy. In a couple of cases, the stories were told to me decades ago, and I have not been able to contact the people involved for clarification. Beyond that, I have strived to tell the tales with as much historical accuracy as possible.

Now please sit back, relax and enjoy the stories. The ghosts have been waiting for you to hear them.

Acknowledgements

I would be lying if I did not say that this book was at least, to some extent, a group effort. From the moment I announced that I was writing it, friends, family, acquaintances and colleagues all stepped out of the woodwork to offer stories, advice and support. Thus, I would like to thank the following, in no particular order:

- My fellow volunteers at the Columbus Landmarks Foundation, through which I got my start in the ghost story telling business. I am particularly grateful to Doreen Uhas Sauer, who is herself a brilliant historian and storyteller; Sandy Lehman; and Tom Betti. Robin Smith, friend and author of her own Columbus ghost story books, was incredibly gracious in offering suggestions on research and stories to pursue.
- Everyone who was kind enough to share their ghost stories with me. There would be no book without you! It has been an honor to document your stories for the enjoyment and wonder of generations to come.
- The Kelton House Museum and Garden. It may seem silly to thank the Kelton ghosts themselves, but they were a huge inspiration. I would not have anywhere near the love I have for history and ghostology if it had not been for them. Thank you to Georgeanne Reuter for giving me permission to write about the house and to Stacey Stiers Herb, Angela Bias and the other house managers and volunteers there for sharing their stories with me.
- My editor, Joe Gartrell, who contacted me out of the blue to write this book. Thank you for giving me such an amazing opportunity!

- RIP Columbus and PARA, the two paranormal investigation groups to which I belong. Not only have they been very supportive, they have been very patient with the fact that I have been an absentee member for the past year.
- The staff and volunteers at the Ohio Historical Society for their research advice and help with many of the illustrations. Duryea Kemp, Lanna Blue and a staff member who wishes to remain nameless (you know who you are!): your aid was greatly appreciated.
- Likewise, Michelle Drobik at The Ohio State University Archives was extremely helpful in selecting photographs for the OSU chapters.
- My husband, Bob, who put up with me working away on the book pretty much every night and weekend for the past year.
- Fellow local historians who shared their knowledge with me and helped clarify some aspects of the history that were muddled. Sandy Andromeda, in particular, cleared up a huge mystery that was driving me nuts.
- My corps of editors and proofreaders: Kara Prem, Lorraine Stephens and especially Jennifer Roth, who helped me polish up the book. I am extremely grateful for all of your suggestions. The book is far better because of them.
- Scott Caputo and the other history librarians at the Columbus Metropolitan Library System, which itself is a phenomenal resource. I hope my fellow Columbusites realize how lucky we are to have it.
- All of my friends who cheered me on and kept telling me how much you were looking forward to reading my book. That really means a lot to me.

INTRODUCTION

A Brief and Somewhat Morbid History of Columbus

Columbus started its life as a manufactured city. It was created to be the capital of Ohio. In the early years of statehood, Ohio was in a bit of a quandary as to where to have its capital city. Chillicothe was the original capital when Ohio became a state in 1803, but other cities such as Zanesville and Worthington were vying for the honor. A group of investors from Franklinton, the original pioneer settlement in the Central Ohio area, came up with a plan to benefit the state. The plan, incidentally, would make them quite rich in the process. They offered to donate to the state land on the high banks of the Scioto River to build the capital there. This gave state legislators an option that not only was centrally located, but it also would not show special favor to any of the established cities. They happily took the investors up on that. Thus, in 1812, Columbus was founded.

The big problem at that point was how to carve a city out of the wilderness. Even the local native tribes had mainly used the area as hunting grounds. The city slowly grew, hampered by poor roads that made importing supplies a difficult undertaking. When taxes weren't enough to fund the needed growth, the city turned to private individuals for loans. Ever frugal, they built the original statehouse from bricks made out of the clay from the ancient Native American mound that had been at Mound and High. The bricks contained bone fragments from the indigenous people buried there. Eventually, the pioneers transformed the roughly hewn settlement into a vibrant city, attracting more new settlers into the area.

That was all threatened when Columbus suffered its first major epidemic with the arrival of cholera in 1833. Between mid-July and the end of September, almost one hundred people lost their lives to the disease. Cholera was so virulent that it wasn't unusual for a perfectly healthy person to catch it in the morning and be dead by the end of the day. That was followed by a smallpox scare ten years later. Cholera made an unwelcome return in 1849 and 1850, killing over five hundred people.

The loss of population and prestige from the epidemics was tempered by the fact that Columbus was becoming a center of commerce. The same year that the first cholera epidemic hit the city, a feeder canal was opened to connect it to the larger canal system throughout the state. That allowed its citizens to easily transport the local produce to markets in other areas. This was preceded in 1831 by the National Road reaching Columbus, making the stagecoach lines owned by tavern keeper William Neil quite lucrative. The era of canals and stagecoaches ended within a few decades with the advent of railroads, but they served their purpose admirably until then.

One aspect of commerce that particularly blossomed in Columbus was the carriage trade. By the end of the 1800s, Columbus boasted two dozen buggy manufacturing companies. An impressive one-sixth of all of the buggies being produced worldwide at that time were made in Columbus, earning the city the moniker of the "Buggy Capital of the World."

Another nickname earned by Columbus during that time period was the Arched City. In 1888, the Grand Army of the Republic, a veterans' association for men who had served in the Union army during the Civil War, decided to hold a reunion in Columbus. About 250,000 people were expected to visit Columbus as a part of that, an overwhelming figure to the city that itself only had a population of 80,000. The highlight of the affair was to be a grand parade down High Street. To help accommodate that, the city lined the path of the parade with gas-lit arches spaced every half a block. In addition to being festive, the added light from the arches proved to be a valuable deterrent to crime there at night. The citizens of Columbus were so enthralled that they insisted that the arches be kept up permanently. While the original arches were taken down long ago, Columbus has once again started installing lighted arches in tribute to this shining part of its history.

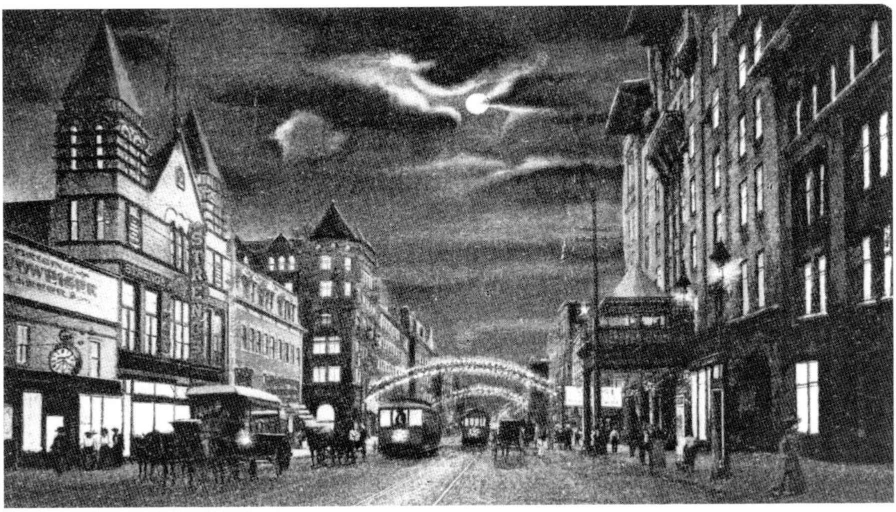

The lighted arches along High Street at the turn of the century gave Columbus the nickname the "Arched City." *Author's collection.*

The year 1913 brought a major tragedy to Columbus. In the couple of days before March 25, heavy rain pelted the city. The levees could not stand the pressure from the swollen Scioto and broke, causing massive flooding in Franklinton. Although flooding was nothing new in the area, they had never dealt with anything of quite this magnitude. Rescue efforts were hampered by the fact that the bridges connecting Franklinton to Columbus were washed out, and the currents were too strong to safely send out rescue parties. By the time the flood had eased, nearly one hundred people were dead and thousands of others homeless.

On April 22, 1930, an even more catastrophic loss of life occurred. At the prison, a fire started in the evening just after the prisoners had been locked in their cells for the night. It grew wildly out of control, killing 322 people in the grossly overcrowded prison. The fire claimed several more lives than "Old Sparky," Ohio's electric chair, did in its sixty-six years as an instrument of execution. The fire was the single largest loss of life in Columbus's history.

After a slowdown in growth during the Great Depression, Columbus's population took a major leap during World War II. Thousands of people from the neighboring states to the south flocked to Columbus to take advantage of wartime manufacturing jobs. Another boost to the population came over the next two decades as a result of the postwar baby boom.

That was tempered by a new and seemingly innocuous threat to the city's population levels: shopping malls. As developers like Don M. Casto built malls in the suburbs surrounding the city, the downtown started to die as a shopping destination. There was less impetus to live close to the heart of the city when one could enjoy newer, more modern amenities out in sparkling suburbia. An attempt in the late 1980s to lure shoppers back to downtown with glamorous, high-end retail shops in the City Center Mall failed miserably.

A further threat to downtown came in the form of freeways. This caused a few issues. First, the construction of the inner belt destroyed large sections of downtown neighborhoods. Thousands of houses and businesses were bulldozed to make way for the highways. This effectively isolated the downtown business district from the residential areas, which had already been dying out downtown. The freeways also made it easier for people to live in the suburbs while still commuting to jobs in the city.

In some ways, it seemed like the suburbs were a danger to the well-being of Columbus proper. Columbus got around that, using a clever little ploy developed during the leadership of Mayor Maynard E. "Jack" Sensenbrenner in the 1950s. In order to use sewer and water hookups from the city, the outlying areas had to allow themselves to be annexed by Columbus. This tactic allowed Columbus to grow "tentacles" around the outlying suburbs, instead of becoming landlocked by them like other large cities in Ohio. Thanks to that, Columbus is now the largest city in the state.

Over the years, Columbus has continued to grow, due in part to its diverse economy. However, there is still an ongoing struggle to balance the past and the future. In the 1960s and '70s, much of Columbus's past was swept away to make room for the modern. The Neil House hotel, which had been situated across the street from the statehouse in one form or another since 1818, was demolished to make way for the Huntington Center. Other historic sites were toppled so that skyscraper office buildings could be erected in their place. Columbus now seems to regret its rash decision to do away with so much of its past. As the city nears its 200th anniversary, there is a push to restore it to the appearance of an earlier era. A row of shops and restaurants spanning Interstate 670 on North High Street was designed to look like the old Union Station train depot that had been torn down to make way for the convention center. New condominiums and apartment buildings are being built to seem as if they had been there for a century. Even some historic downtown buildings such as the Seneca Hotel and the Hartman Building have been renovated to lure new residents who appreciate things of the past.

Not that they needed to worry that Columbus's past would ever be completely forgotten. The many ghosts of this city will always be around to remind us.

Death in Old Columbus

You know life is hard when editorials in the local newspapers complain about how many people keep dying. That was the case in 1824, when Philo H. Olmsted, editor of the *Columbus Gazette*, wrote, "We are encompassed with accidents ever ready to crush the moldering tenements that we inhabit. The seeds of disease are planted in our constitution by the hand of nature… We see our friends and neighbors perishing around us."

When looking at the mortality index for Franklin County from 1860, one is sobered by the number of people who went to their graves before reaching their fiftieth birthdays. What is particularly striking is the percentage of people who died under the age of five. Roughly one-quarter of the deaths listed were of young children. Scarlet fever in particular took a big toll on them. Others died from curiously named diseases such as "summer complaint," which was a form of cholera, and the mysterious "information brain."

Things did not improve much over the next sixty years. Before a cure was found in the mid-twentieth century, syphilis could be a death sentence to entire families, killing even the children who were born after a parent contracted it. One is likewise struck by the number of suicides found in early twentieth-century death records. Men were much more likely to commit suicide than women, and their preferred method was death by shotgun. Death by being struck by a train was surprisingly common, even among people who weren't railroad workers. One of the most prevalent causes of death in adults in both periods was consumption, known today as tuberculosis.

While the average lifespan in earlier time periods was much lower than it is today, many people did still live to a ripe old age. It isn't unusual to find people in the 1860 mortality index who died in their late seventies and eighties. One man even made it to ninety-eight years of age.

One might note that in the early days of Columbus, the dead never seemed to stay buried. There were originally three cemeteries: the North Graveyard on what is now the southeast corner of Park and Spruce Streets, the South Graveyard on Livingston Road and the Catholic Cemetery at Washington and Mount Vernon Avenues. There was also the old pioneer

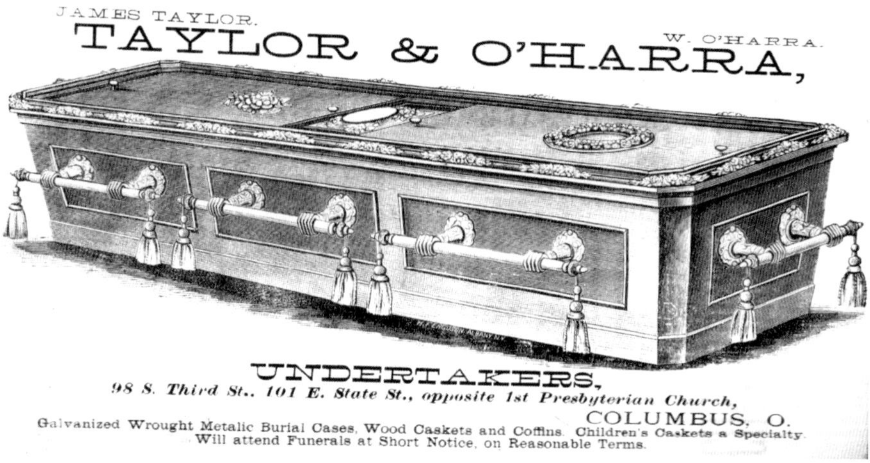

Funerals and their trappings became increasingly elaborate throughout the nineteenth century. *Courtesy of the Columbus Metropolitan Library.*

cemetery in Franklinton. Over the years, as land values became higher, there developed a correspondingly higher concern over the health issues involved in having dead bodies buried so close to populated areas. In 1848, Green Lawn Cemetery was established south of Franklinton. Compared to the earlier cemeteries, which were basically burial yards, Green Lawn Cemetery was luxurious. It was designed with the newer sensibilities that cemeteries should be restful, parklike places that even the living would enjoy coming to visit.

In 1856, Columbus passed an ordinance making it illegal to bury bodies in the old city graveyards. Green Lawn Cemetery offered to exchange burial plots for the ones in the city graveyards and reinter the bodies there. Further pressure was on to remove the bodies entirely when railroad companies expressed interest in owning the land occupied by the North Graveyard. This caused some issues. The families of many of the deceased, especially those buried in the Catholic graveyard, felt that it was sacrilegious to move the bodies. They filed lawsuits against it. As the years passed and the legal issues regarding that were slowly worked out, some confusion developed as to which bodies had already been moved and which were still left in the Catholic Cemetery. As a result, bodies got left behind. Human skeletons are occasionally uncovered when the grounds are dug up around Columbus State Community College, which is on the site of the old Catholic Cemetery.

Franklinton Cemetery did not fare much better, although the majority of the bodies stayed in place. The remains of the early city leaders such as Lucas Sullivant and Lyne Starling, along with their families, were relocated to the more chichi Green Lawn Cemetery. When care of the graveyard was passed on to the Franklin Township trustees after the Civil War, and later to the City of Columbus, they were apparently not as concerned about it now that the most prestigious denizens had been disinterred. By the early 1900s, the cemetery had fallen into an extreme state of neglect and was being used as a hobo camp. Thankfully, in recent years, efforts have been made to restore the Franklinton Cemetery. It is once again a pleasant resting place for Columbus's oldest settlers.

Even if one's remains were not relocated to a different cemetery, there was always the possibility that one's body might be stolen by "resurrection men." Columbus was home to many medical colleges over the years, all of which needed corpses for teaching purposes. Demand was understandably higher than supply. As early as 1839, grave robbing had become such a problem that a watchman was hired to keep vigil at the North Graveyard. By 1846, grave robbing was still so widespread that legislation was introduced to require medical practitioners to enter into bonds not to violate the laws against it. Still, that did not stop the grave robbers. After the Civil War, the demand for cadavers was so great that organized gangs were hired to fill orders for dozens of bodies at a time.

Some people went to elaborate lengths to prevent the disturbance of their loved ones' graves. In addition to fortifying the actual grave by placing the coffins in vaults or putting heavy stones on top of them, one unusual theft prevention device was the "Clover Coffin Torpedo." This was placed in the grave and would explode if disturbed.

The resurrection men were savvy enough to pick the graveyards that would be the easiest to steal from. The cemeteries of the Ohio State Penitentiary and the Columbus State Hospital were favorite targets. Even this infuriated the citizens. In 1839, an angry mob stormed the Worthington Reformed Medical College over growing suspicions that the faculty had been robbing paupers' graves in Columbus. Not surprisingly, they found bodies that had recently gone missing.

When the dead are not allowed to rest in peace, is it any wonder that Columbus is so haunted?

CHAPTER 1
FORGOTTEN SOULS
FRANKLIN COUNTY POOR HOUSE

Most kids secretly think of school as a form of jail. Thus, it was no surprise to the children at Beck Street Elementary School when balls and chains were unearthed from under the parking lot while workmen were doing repairs on it.

The grownups were shocked.

It is hard to imagine that this quaint, upscale German Village neighborhood could have ever been the site of the Franklin County Poor House, one of the saddest, most forgotten institutions in Columbus's history.

The story began before Columbus was even a city. In earlier times, it was expected that one's extended family would look out for those who were less fortunate. That posed a problem on the Ohio frontier where so many of the pioneers had left their families behind back in the east. The Northwest Territories made it the legal responsibility of the township trustees to care for the poor and gave them the right to levy taxes for it. This responsibility was transferred to the counties after Ohio attained statehood. As tends to be the case, they allowed the counties to farm the care of the poor out to the lowest bidders. The lowest bids often resulted in the lowest quality of care, so the legislators continued to look for a better solution.

In 1831, the counties were authorized by the Ohio legislature to operate poorhouses to care for the less fortunate. The Franklin County commissioners decided to buy a farm at the fork of the Scioto and Olentangy Rivers for this purpose. That ended up being inadequate for their needs. The site was three miles north of Columbus, making it awkward to get there. That was exacerbated by problems crossing the rivers when they were high. The poorhouse was designed to handle only nine or ten inmates, and it soon became apparent that there was a greater demand than that. The commissioners decided to move the county poorhouse to the south end of Columbus. The south end at that time was considered to be less desirable real estate in general, full of smelly businesses such as breweries and tanneries. The commissioners purchased a five-acre lot between Beck and Sycamore Streets in 1839 and later expanded that by another six acres in 1844. They put up several buildings on the site over the years.

Unfortunately, even with the improved physical circumstances, the quality of life at the poorhouse was what historian William E. Kappes described as "benign neglect." In 1850, the Ohio legislature tried to mitigate the public impression of the poorhouses statewide by changing their name to county infirmaries. Of course, most people still referred to them as poorhouses regardless. The City of Columbus did erect a city hospital near the Franklin County Infirmary grounds in 1845, putting it under the supervision of the infirmary's superintendent. However, while there was a greater emphasis on care for the infirm, the poorhouses were still used as homes for the indigent. Their records confirm that. In the intake records from 1867, one can see inmates listed as suffering from the disease of being "poor," as well as more physical maladies of syphilis, lunacy, tuberculosis and being in the "family way." As late as 1895, the *Columbus Evening Dispatch* still mentioned that state law did not allow children over the age of three to stay in the poorhouses out of concern that they would be raised in "an atmosphere of poverty."

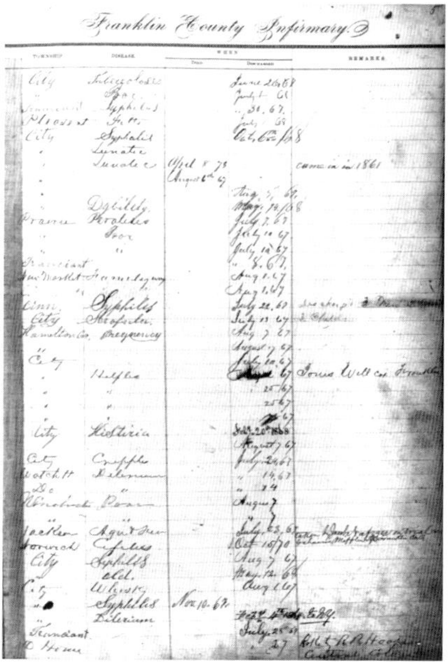

The Franklin County Infirmary intake ledger lists inmates suffering from poverty, as well as insanity, pregnancy and tuberculosis. *Courtesy of the Ohio Historical Society.*

In some cases, the living conditions were downright scary. In a report from the State Board of Charities in 1868, they cite that the Franklin County Infirmary was designed to hold 200 people. At one point during the reporting period, the infirmary was up to 237 inmates. By the end of the reporting period, they were down to a more comfortable 166 inmates. However, 53 of those were insane. Even more disturbing is the fact that they had only fourteen cells to hold the insane, the cells themselves being only five by seven feet each.

The living conditions for the insane were particularly horrific. The report describes many of them as living on the upper floor of a building. Their cells did not have windows, for fear patients might harm themselves on them. Instead, the only light in that floor was provided by a single small window at either end of the hallway. The report goes on to tell a very sad tale about the inhabitants of some of the cells:

> *Through one of these windows the light of the strong August sun was barely sufficient to discover the interior and reveal the condition of the inmates of one of these cells. In it were confined a maniac and idiot. The latter, entirely nude, was crouching, mid his own filth, in one corner of the cell, while the mad-man stood grasping the strong timbers of the door—now raving wildly, and anon entreating mildly, for deliverance from his terrible thralldom. In an opposite cell, furious in his madness, which literally "no man could tame," was another inmate, who, seven years ago, had been transferred from the Ohio Penitentiary.*

The report notes that the Franklin County Infirmary had been charged with caring for an unusually high percentage of insane inmates due to its proximity to the State Insane Asylum and the Ohio Penitentiary. That was a task for which it had not been designed and was ill prepared to handle. Two years later, the State Board of Charities also noted the poor physical condition of the facilities in general. In both reports, they credit the superintendent and staff as having done the best they could with the resources they had. However, they chastised the local government by saying, "The welfare and protection of one hundred and seventy inmates, unfortunate and needy though they be, can not be a matter of indifference to the people of the county."

With that, plans were made to move the Franklin County Infirmary to another site just outside of the city limits. It was to be on the west end of King Avenue along the Olentangy River. That fell through, and a new infirmary was eventually built on Eberle Road, which is now Alum Creek Drive. The Franklin County Infirmary closed down the Beck Street site between 1883 and 1884. The City of Columbus wasted no time in putting the land to another use. In 1884, they opened on the site the Beck Street

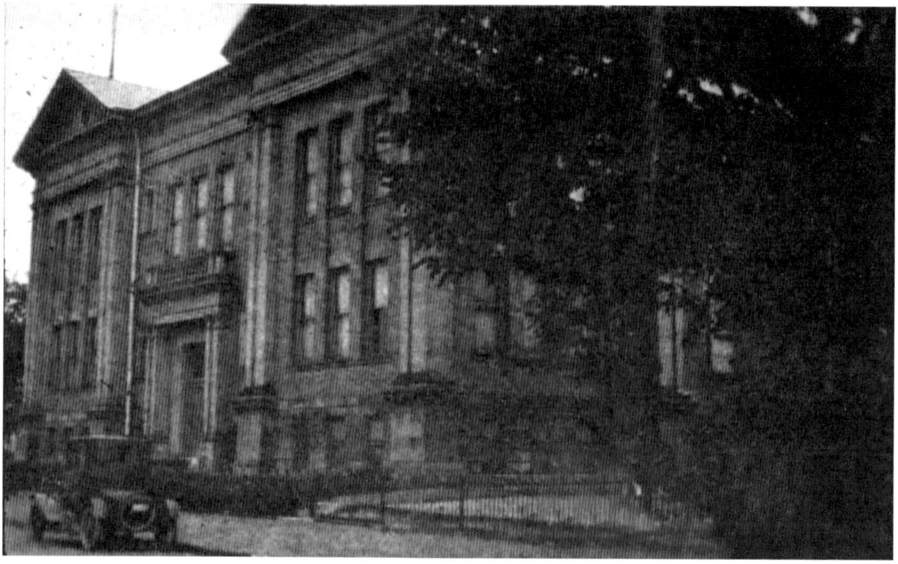

The Beck Street Elementary School was built on the site of the second Franklin County Poor House. *Courtesy of Columbus Metropolitan Library.*

Elementary School, now called Livingston Elementary School. The rest of the property was divided up into residential lots. Poor House Lane, which had run through the center of the property, was renamed Lathrop Lane, and all traces of the old poorhouse were swept away in the name of progress.

Or so they thought.

While the poorhouse and its inmates are long forgotten in the communal memory of the people of Columbus, every now and then remnants resurface to remind us of its existence. The most striking reminder was the unearthing of the balls and chains under the Beck Street Elementary School parking lot in the mid-1960s. However, some local residents live with a daily reminder.

Sharon Harper grew up in a house built on the property. She remembers her house and some other ones in the neighborhood as being rather odd. One of the neighbor's houses in particular had a feature that one doesn't normally see in the real estate listings: jail cells in the basement! It turns out that the house was partially built on the foundation of one of the several buildings that made up the infirmary. Sharon thought that the neighbor was joking when she first heard about the cells, but then the neighbor invited her over to see. Sure enough, there were several cells down there "just large enough to fit in a small bed and a chamber pot." It is unclear as to whether these were actually used to hold prisoners during their stays at the infirmary or if they were the normal living quarters of the common inmates. Either way, they are sad reminders of how dismal life there must have been.

Sharon's house had its own peculiar feature: an extra resident that no one could see. The first time that she knew something was up was when she was home by herself on the first floor and heard heavy footsteps walking around on the floor above her. Over time, other people heard the footsteps, too. Eventually, her friends refused to come over to visit because they were afraid of the noises they heard in the house. As one friend put it, "This house is so damn weird!"

Even if one could get used to the footsteps, sometimes the ghost was harder to ignore. One time Sharon and her mother heard the sound of someone running down the stairs into the dining room where they were. They looked up at the stairs when they heard the racket, but no one was there. Not surprisingly, a dog they had would not go near that stairwell. Every time they tried to get him to go near it, he would cower and whine in fear.

Sharon's father was a skeptic when it came to ghosts, but he had an experience that he couldn't brush off. He was sitting in a room near some of the built-in cabinets that graced the house. As he was sitting there, the cabinet doors swung open. He wasn't bothered by that. To his practical mind, someone must have left them slightly ajar and a combination of gravity and an unbalanced hang on the hinges caused the movement. He got up and closed them. Just within the few steps it took to get back to his seat, the doors had swung open again. This was a bit more perplexing. He knew darn well that he had shut the doors firmly. Still, he chalked it up to a fluke. He shut the doors again. By the time he had gotten back to his seat, the doors had swung open a third time. He decided that if some unseen person wanted the doors open that badly, he would leave them be.

The curious effects of the poorhouse seemed to spill over the boundaries of the site. New neighbors moved in across the street from Sharon. They had a Great Dane. While he wasn't a bad dog, he was like a bull in a china shop. The neighbors decided that it would be smart to leave him locked up in the basement while they were at work. The first day they came home, they found the dog loose upstairs and the basement door torn off its hinges. This was a solidly built old house, and it would have taken a great deal of energy for the dog, even as big as he was, to have managed that. The neighbors assumed that the dog was just nervous about being in a new environment and had knocked the door down during a panic attack. They fixed the door and tried to reassure the dog that he was safe in his new home. The next day, they put him back in the basement. That evening, they once more came home to find the door ripped from it hinges and the dog upstairs. After the dog broke the door down a few times, the neighbors gave up on keeping him down there.

The dog's overwhelming fear of the basement did not make much sense to them until one night when they were shooting the breeze with the other neighbors. When they mentioned the problem with the dog, the neighbors became quiet and gave each other knowing looks. The neighbors said that a little girl and her aunt had previously lived there. The aunt committed suicide by hanging herself in the basement. That explained another strange occurrence down there. They had noticed that the light in the basement would turn itself on at certain times of the day. Sharon's new neighbors moved out within a year.

One cannot definitively say that a ghostly inmate from the poorhouse was responsible for the strange happenings at Sharon's house or that residual sadness from it drove a nearby resident to the point of suicide. However, it does seem likely. Anyone who has ever felt the lingering tension in an empty room just after an argument took place knows that emotions stay around after the people have left. When there have been several decades of intense, tormented emotions occurring on one site, one can see how that might permeate the atmosphere of the area. And when the long-dead inmates there lived lives beneath the notice of the average man, it makes sense that they might be hungry for a little attention from beyond the grave.

CHAPTER 2

SCHOOL SPIRITS

THE OHIO STATE UNIVERSITY

The Ohio State University, originally named the Ohio Agricultural and Mechanical College, opened on September 17, 1873, to a coed class of twenty-five students and little fanfare. The *Columbus Dispatch* didn't even mention it except to quote President Edward Orton's comments on a lawsuit to allow young women to attend. Indeed, it was off to a modest start. The main building was not even finished when classes started.

In truth, the "main" building, eventually known as University Hall, was the only building when the university opened. It was a full-service structure, providing facilities for classes, laboratories, dormitories for the male students, faculty living quarters, a dining hall and the library. With all that human activity, it was a lively place.

Even back then, the students were as high spirited as they are today. A favorite prank was played by the students in the middle of the night. The young men, dressed in their night shirts with their pillows clutched in one hand, would form a train and walk up to an upper floor to knock on the resident professor's door. When the weary academic poked his head out to find out what they wanted, they would pelt him with a barrage of pillows.

When the university first opened, it had a comfortable ratio of seven instructors to its twenty-five students. By 1881, President Reverend Walter Q. Scott lamented that "many classes were too large to be thoroughly taught." The growing enrollment also led to him pressing the board of trustees to establish a dorm for the female students, whose ranks had grown to forty-one. Up to that point, the female students lived either with

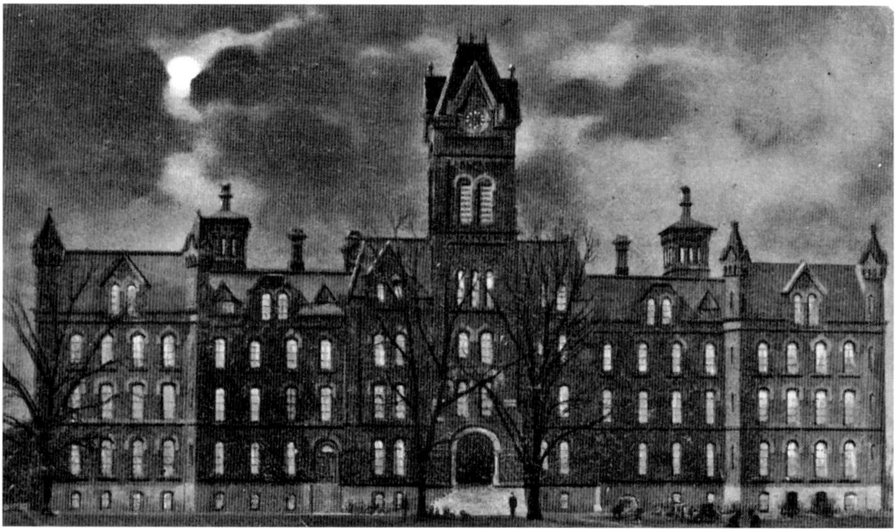

University Hall was the only building on The Ohio State University's campus when it first opened. *Author's collection.*

family or in nearby rooming houses. It took a while to convince the trustees of the need. The first women's dorm was finally built in 1906 under the tenure of President William Oxley Thompson. It was named Oxley Hall in honor of his mother.

In the meanwhile, the old North Dorm had fallen into disrepair to the extent that it was abandoned in favor of a new building. The building trend continued from there. Over the years, student housing at Ohio State has expanded to forty residence halls. Some unusual buildings have been pressed into service as dormitories as well. In order to help financially disadvantaged students during the Great Depression, part of the Ohio Stadium was renovated for use as a cooperative dormitory. The west side of the stadium stayed in use as student housing for several decades.

It is hard to tell how many students died in the dorms over the years. The Ohio State University did not keep track of the deaths until the 1980s. Whatever the number, there were apparently plenty.

One exceptionally disturbing set of deaths occurred in the winter of 1925. On January 31, senior Charles H. Huls, editor of the *Makio* student yearbook, succumbed to what was first attributed to tetanus. A junior, David J. Pushkin, died the next day of possible meningitis. In short order, three more students fell ill with convulsions and symptoms similar to those that had killed the young men. Thankfully, the true cause of their illness was found in time for them to be saved. Upon investigation, it was discovered that all five of the students had taken quinine cold capsules dispensed by the College of Pharmacy. The capsules in their possession were found to contain strychnine.

Inquiries were made by the university, the Columbus police and a special investigation instituted by the governor. At first, the university was reluctant to believe that it could have been done on purpose. Huls's death certificate states his cause of death as "accidental strychnine poisoning." University officials likewise made comments trying to excuse the pharmacy professors for not supervising the pharmacy students closely enough. The accidental poisoning theory seemed less likely once a bottle of strychnine was found hidden where it didn't belong in the pharmacy. Newspapers latched on to the story with ghoulish hyperbole, touting the murderer as a "master criminal" and "super-intellectual with a maniacal desire to broadcast death." Master criminal or not, the killer was smart enough to escape justice. Despite the efforts of the investigations, the culprit was never found.

While there aren't any known hauntings relating to the poisoning case, The Ohio State University has no shortage of ghostly goings-on. South Campus in particular seems to be a center of activity. Canfield Hall, a women's dorm on South Campus, is said to be haunted. It opened in the fall of 1940; an additional wing was built in 1954, forming a courtyard with Mack Hall. A lot of people have felt very uncomfortable in the courtyard at night, being overwhelmed with feelings of pain and sadness. There have been reports of an apparition walking around there. Inside is not much better. It is common for the young women living there to hear footsteps walking around their beds at night and have a strong sensation of being watched.

The attic of Pomerene Hall also has a spirit. In the late 1990s, some student workers were sent up to the attic to put away AV (audio/visual) equipment. They were surprised to run into a man in Victorian clothing up there and were even more surprised when he faded away.

The buildings weren't the only places that had spooks. An alumnus who went to school at Ohio State in the early 1980s had an odd story about the west lawn of the Ohio Union:

> *While I was a student there, I spent a lot of time at the Ohio Union at night. A couple of other psychically sensitive friends and I often felt presences hanging around on the lawn to the west of the building when we were leaving for the evening. When we compared notes, we inevitably found that each of us was sensing the same number of presences in the same area.*

> *It varied from night to night. Sometimes there would just be a couple, and other times there would be over a dozen.*
>
> *It never occurred to us that they were ghosts. Who expects ghosts to be hanging out on the campus lawn? We weren't really sure what the heck they were. We were all heavily into science fiction and thought that maybe we were sensing some beings from an alternate universe that somehow overlapped with ours. It wasn't unusual to feel them in the back seat of the car hitching a ride home with us afterwards. We never felt threatened by them. They just seemed kind of curious about us.*

There may be more to that than just their imagination. There are human remains interred on campus. The ashes of former student and trustee Herbert "Hub" Atkinson are imbedded in Bricker Hall on South Campus, not far from the west lawn of the Ohio Union. Others are said to be buried in the Oval lawn itself.

North Campus is not without its tales, either. A strange series of events happened to Nigel Willoughby (name changed upon request) and his roommate one fall quarter in the late 1990s. They were living in a dorm room in Taylor Tower that apparently came with an extra roommate.

Not long after they moved in, they noticed that items around the dorm room would be moved when they were out. At first, each assumed that the other had been moving the objects. When one would check with his roommate to find out why things kept being moved, the other would deny having anything to do with it.

If Nigel and his roommate had any doubts that the other was playing a prank by moving the objects, those doubts were removed when the objects started moving in front of them. They would be sitting around watching TV when a pen sitting on the TV stand would start sliding several inches by itself.

The poltergeist evidently preferred showier displays of its abilities. Its new trick was to throw things around. Nigel was amazed one day to see a bottle opener jump off the shelf. While it was plausible that vibrations from people walking around the dorm could have jiggled a small object to fall off a shelf, the bottle opener had been sitting several inches from the edge when it fell. Even harder to explain away was the time when a corkboard that had been nailed on to the wall mysteriously jumped off of the wall in front of Nigel's eyes. Eventually, Nigel took the strange occurrences for granted. Weeks later, when he was fixing a bowl of ramen noodles for lunch, a figurine leaped off the shelf. It bonked him in the forehead and then knocked into his bowl, spilling it all over the floor. Rather than be amazed at what happened, Nigel was put out over the loss of his lunch.

The roommates were understandably curious about their invisible friend. They were not able to find any evidence that anyone had ever died in the room. Their only clue was a muffled woman's voice that they heard from time to time. Considering that they lived on an all-male floor, women's voices were not a common sound. Even if one of their neighbors had a female guest over, the woman's voice they heard in their room was not muffled to the same degree that they could hear through the walls. They weren't sure what to make of it.

The spirit seemed to enjoy attention. When Nigel and his roommate had friends over, the poltergeist would move things in front of the whole gang. Nigel's roommate was particularly intrigued by the activity. He would egg the ghost on, asking her to move things around in front of him. She happily complied. Another time, they had a party in their room. There were several balloons left over from it that they left lying on the floor when they went to bed. In the middle of the night, they heard the balloons popping in quick succession.

Late in the quarter, they awoke one morning to find an inch of water on the floor. This, however, was not a part of the spirit's shenanigans. A wave of winter weather had come through town overnight, freezing a water pipe and causing it to burst. Maintenance men were called in to fix the pipes and clean up the mess. In the process, they removed a ventilation grill from the wall. There, tucked back in the vent, they found a faded Polaroid photograph. It showed a college-aged woman walking through a field with a dog. Her hair and clothing looked to be from a time about twenty years earlier. Nigel and his roommate were mystified by the photograph having been left there and wondered if maybe the young woman was their unseen friend. They kept the photograph for awhile but threw it out when they went home for winter break. When they came back the next quarter, they found that the ghostly activity had stopped. After thinking about it, it occurred to them that nothing strange had happened since they found the photograph.

It seems that neither the living nor the dead can resist staying around their old alma mater. The alumni keep coming back to visit, and the spirits never leave.

CHAPTER 3

THE HOUSE OF SECRETS

KELTON HOUSE MUSEUM AND GARDEN

Nestled in the heart of a quiet neighborhood in downtown Columbus is a house of secrets. Unlike its opulent Victorian neighbors, the Kelton House Museum and Garden does not draw attention to itself. It has a quiet, almost demure facade. That serves to hide its intrigues well. Few would guess that, among other things, behind the unpretentious walls lies one of the most haunted houses in Columbus.

From the very beginning, the Kelton House was designed to keep certain things hidden. Fernando Cortez Kelton and his wife, Sophia, were ardent abolitionists who used their home as a safe house for runaway slaves on the Underground Railroad. At the time they built it in 1852, their Town Street mansion was considered to be way out in the country, separated from the heart of downtown by a swamp. That might have been calculated to give them more privacy to carry out their clandestine activities. Another feature of the house that would have come in handy for this is the belvedere, which would have allowed them to scan the countryside for any incoming escapees. Due to the secret nature of the activities, it is not known how many escaped slaves they helped over the years. However, they were apparently well thought of for their abolitionist work. The Keltons were so respected that Fernando was given the honor of being one of the pallbearers at the funeral procession for Abraham Lincoln when his body was brought to Columbus on its way home to Illinois.

The Keltons were originally from New England. When Fernando came to Columbus, he started working for A.P. Stone in his dry goods business.

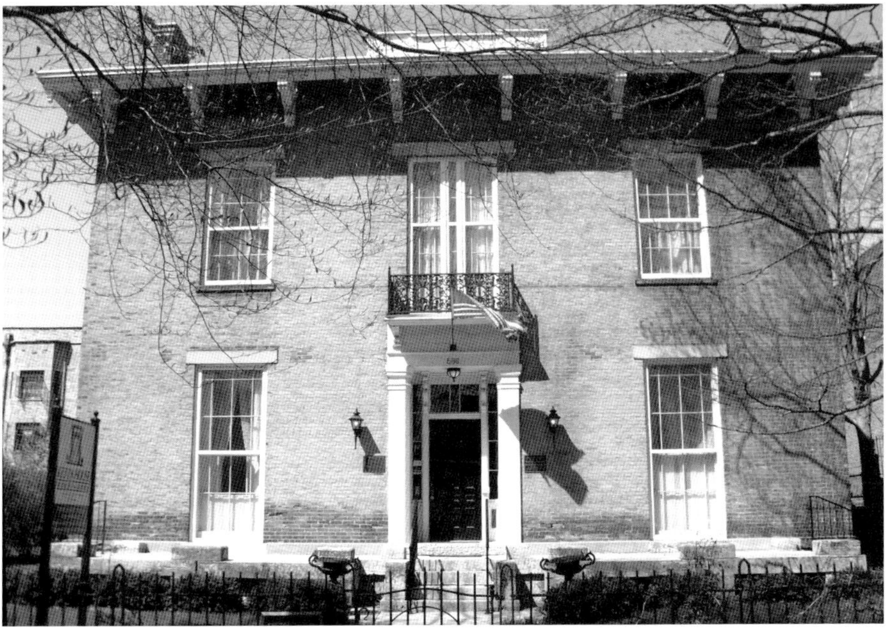

The Kelton House was home to a family of abolitionists who used it as a stop on the Underground Railroad. *Author's collection.*

He soon fell in love with Sophia Langdon Stone, his boss's pretty sister. They married in 1841. Fernando moved on to start his own wholesale dry goods and pharmaceutical business, the Kelton and Bancroft Company. The business prospered, and their family grew large. They had seven children altogether, losing only one to a childhood illness. In an era when one in four children died before reaching adulthood, they were fairly lucky.

Their luck ran out with the Civil War, which brought both a double tragedy and an unexpected new member to the family. First, eldest son Oscar believed that it was his duty to join the army to fight slavery. His parents reluctantly gave him their permission once he was of legal age and had finished the school year at Kenyon College. He joined the Ninety-fifth Ohio Volunteer Infantry in August 1862 and was immediately made a corporal. By the time he was killed less than two years later at the Battle of Brice's Crossroads, he had worked his way up to first lieutenant. By all accounts, he was a brave soldier and a fair and decent officer. One touching story involves a reunion dinner held by the regiment after the war had ended. A place was set at the table for Oscar, adorned with white flowers and a place card giving him the honorary title of captain.

The same year that he died, Sophia Kelton discovered a couple of young runaway slave girls hiding in the bushes near the house. They were around eleven and twelve, roughly the same age as some of her own children. The girls were anxious to get on to Canada, but Martha, the younger of the two Hartway sisters, was very ill. Her sister went on without her, leaving her in the care of the Keltons. Martha stayed with them until her marriage a decade later. Indications are that she was raised as a member of the family, which would have been quite an unusual situation for that time period. Martha remained close to the Keltons throughout her life, even naming her children after a couple of her Kelton siblings.

After the war had ended, Fernando Kelton made the sad trip down to Guntown, Mississippi, to retrieve his son's body. On the way back, the wagon was jolted by a bump in the road so hard that Fernando fell out. He hit his head on a rock, which left him knocked out for a few days. He recovered and was able to make the trip home. Unfortunately, the injury to his head caused him to have severe dizzy spells occasionally. Not long after, when he was in his third-floor office in the fashionable Gwynn Building downtown, one of his dizzy spells struck. He stuck his head out of the window in hopes that the fresh air might quell the dizziness. Instead, he lost his balance completely and fell out of the window. He died from his injuries a few days later.

The next generation of the family brought in a fresh wave of independent thinking in the form of Belle Coit. She was a spirited suffragist who married Frank Kelton, Sophia and Fernando's youngest son. Belle had a good upbringing for suffragism. She was the daughter of Elizabeth Coit, a leading women's rights activist in Columbus in the mid-1800s. Belle was an instigator of change. When Ohio State University opened in 1873, Belle and her female friends sued the state legislature to allow them to attend. She remained active in her fight for women's rights until she died just short of her 101st birthday in 1956.

Grace, Sophia and Fernando's granddaughter through son Edwin, was likewise a trailblazer. In the early 1900s at the age of seventeen, she went by herself to New York City to study art at the Pratt Institute. After coming back to Columbus to teach for a bit, she returned to New York to study interior design at the Parson School of Design. She became one of the first people in the nation to make a living as an interior decorator. Her business got off to a good start when Prescott Bush, grandfather of President George Bush, became her first client. The highlight of her prestigious career came in the early 1960s when she was invited by Jacqueline Kennedy, as a part of a committee of the Association of Interior Decorators, to redecorate two of the rooms in the White House.

The Kelton House owes its continued existence to Grace's strong will. When the government was first looking into building the Interstate 71 freeway, the original plan was to have it go right through where the Kelton House stands. Grace fought to have the freeway moved over by one block. Fearing what would happen to her beloved home after she died, Grace left it in her will to the Columbus Foundation. The stipulation was that they had to either find someone to turn it into a center for learning within six months or it was to be torn down and made into a park for the city. Thankfully, the Junior League of Columbus, committed to Grace Kelton's vision, restored the home to its 1850s look and created a museum. They spent several years and hundreds of thousands of dollars to turn it into a museum of Victorian life.

It's hard to estimate the exact number of spirits dwelling there, but based on the number of full-bodied apparition sightings, there are quite a few. Various folks have reported seeing Grace herself, to a little girl, to genteel ladies in Civil War–era gowns, to burly Union officers holding a meeting in the delicately feminine sitting room.

The earliest spirit is Oscar Kelton, the young soldier. He is usually seen still in his uniform, standing outside the house smoking. This can cause some concern to the neighbors, many of whom keep a protective eye on the house. House manager Angela Bias was setting up the house for a wedding on a Saturday afternoon when a neighbor telephoned to let her know that there was a young man loitering around the side of the building smoking. Angela went outside to shoo him off but there was nobody there. She assumed that he had just been passing through and had left on his own. Fifteen minutes later, the neighbor called up a second time. "There's a man outside, and he's smoking!" she reported. Angela and her coworker both looked around the perimeter of the house but did not find the culprit. Not too long after that, the neighbor called yet again, distressed that the man was still there. This time, Angela kept the neighbor on the phone while she sent the coworker out to look around. The coworker did her reconnaissance and then yelled through the side door that she didn't see anyone around. When Angela relayed that back over the phone, the neighbor was incredulous. "What do you mean?" she asked. "He is standing right beside her!"

Angela's sister, Stacey Herb, has had her own sightings. She spent many evenings there waiting to close up while the Junior League held meetings back in the carriage house. Her favorite perch was the foot of the stairs in

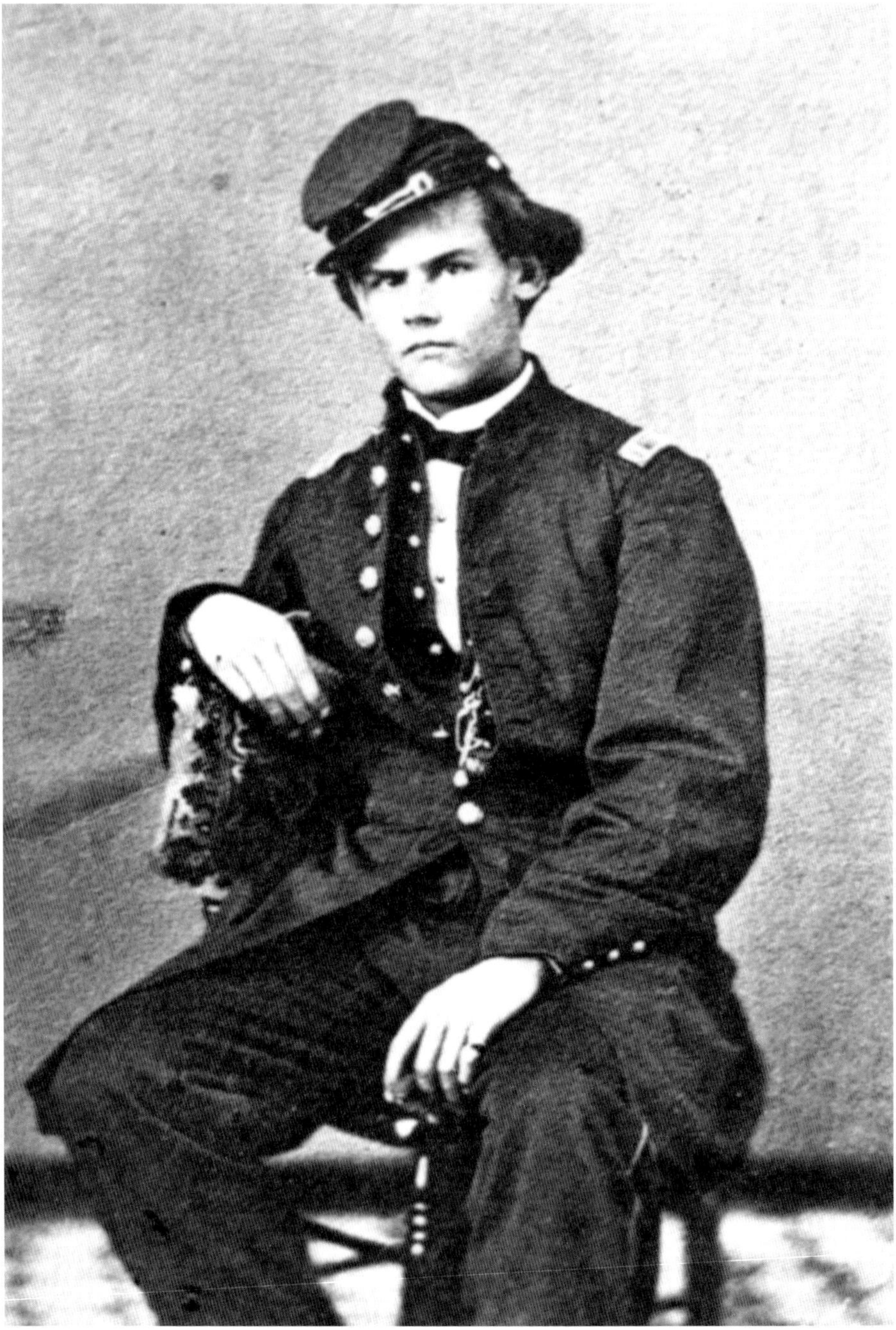

Lieutenant Oscar Dwight Kelton is one of the most frequently seen spirits at the Kelton House Museum and Garden. *Ohio Historical Society.*

the grand hallway, roughly across from the back parlor. While she was sitting there, it wasn't unusual for her to see a blonde woman in a burgundy bustle gown pacing back and forth anxiously in the parlor. Instead of being an interactive spirit, this one seems to be a playback of an intensely emotional scene that somehow recorded itself into the fabric of reality.

The identity of this spirit is not certain, but it is likely that she is Anna Kelton, the eldest child of Sophia and Fernando. She lived there with her mother during the 1870s and 1880s when bustles were in fashion. Anna had a series of hard years before that. Following the loss of her brother and father within such a short time, her own beloved husband died after they had only been married a couple of years. It is easy to imagine that she may have been so distressed at some point that it forever etched itself into the memory of the walls.

While that particular haunting may be an imprint in time, there is one troubled soul in the house. Over the years, there have been some reports of people sensing a spirit who is not in the best of moods. The staff was alerted to this early on when they decided to have a Halloween party in the house in the 1980s. A fortuneteller was stationed in the attic to give those who wanted a reading more privacy. Fifteen minutes after he set up, he came back down, saying that he couldn't work up there because there was a very angry spirit around. Others have reported a similar feeling. The sense of anger seems to be directed only at men who encroach upon his territory, though. The area is now used as a changing room for the female docents, who lead tours of the house in period attire. While they sometimes sense a presence up there, it is benign.

So who is the ghost in the attic? He is generally believed to be Arthur Kelton, the enigma of the family. Arthur, the second to the youngest child of Sophia and Fernando, was restless even in life. After working as a clerk for several years at both his family's and another company, he went into business as a landscape photographer with W.H. Gates. That association only lasted a year. Next, he moved to New York, where he worked as a printer. There he married Maggie Dewitt of Ontario, Canada. Wanderlust caught up with him again, so he moved to Colorado and resumed a career as a photographer. From there, it gets confusing. A family history written by his nephew states that while he was in Colorado, his wife died. It says he then caught mountain fever and moved back to Columbus, where he died around 1914. However, the same history notes that Arthur's son, Frank, moved to San Diego after World War I to be with his mother, Maggie, who died in 1937. Arthur's death certificate and cemetery records indicate he died in 1930. The cemetery records contain yet another mystery about Arthur. Never one to stay in one place, Arthur's body was moved from its original spot to a different one in the family plot in Green Lawn Cemetery a couple of decades after he died.

Many docents have reported feeling a gust of wind whoosh through the attic door as soon as they opened it, as if someone were trying to get out. Logically, that could be blamed on a draft coming down from the belvedere. However, another docent has had a recurring experience that is harder to explain. She unlocked the deadbolted attic door, shut it behind her and went off into a side room that was used as the docents' dressing room. When she came back out, she found that the deadbolt was now sticking out, holding the door open. The only way the bolt could have been left in that position would be if she had turned the key 180 degrees to open the door, then turned it back a full 360 degrees the other way. That isn't the kind of movement one makes accidentally, even in a moment of absentmindedness.

Despite the eeriness of the attic, the house in general has a happy feeling to it. The ghosts love Halloween and are at their mischievous best during the ghost tours given by the Columbus Landmarks Foundation every October. During one tour, a guest asked the docents, who were dressed in Civil War–era mourning gowns, if she could take their picture. She had the two of them nicely framed in her viewfinder while they were standing on the stairs. She took the picture and looked back up to thank them. She was confused to see that there was only one docent standing there. When she looked back at the picture she had just taken, it showed the one docent and a bunch of little sparkles where the other "docent" had been.

They have a running joke involving a couple of dolls in a little bed in the upstairs hallway. Ghostly hands have flipped the dolls over to lie face down a couple of years in a row during the ghost tours. The first year it happened, it occurred just before the tours were about to begin. Coincidentally, a few minutes beforehand, the docents had been trading some last-minute ghost stories, one of which involved an earlier incident with the dolls flipping over. The next year, a news crew came to do a haunted house story and made a big fuss over the dolls. The ghosts apparently liked the attention from that. A few nights later, the docent told the story from the previous year and suggested that the guests keep an eye on the dolls. Then they all moved into a bedroom to hear more stories there. When they came out, a guest screamed and pointed at the dolls. The dolls were both now lying face down. A tour staff member who had been standing in the doorway right next to the dolls swore that no one had touched them. The next night, another docent was working. Not knowing what had happened on the night before, she was surprised to see the dolls lying face down when she came in. At the end of the evening, she went back to turn off the lights and was even more surprised to find that one of the dolls was lying face up. The following year, the dolls flipped over three times during Halloween week. On the final night, the ghosts decided to tease everyone by flipping a doll in a nearby baby carriage instead of the ones in the bed as expected.

The Kelton spirits have a sense of humor about themselves, too. After a ghost played a prank on one of the docents, she chided it by calling it "Sillypants." A male voice quickly popped into her head correcting her with "That's Lieutenant Sillypants!"

There seems to be a mutual admiration between the Keltons and the museum staff. The staff is fiercely protective of the ghosts, not allowing paranormal investigations there, for fear of making them feel "like bugs under a microscope." In turn, the ghosts tend to play with the staff members who are the most appreciative of their antics. During one shift, a house manager heard a loud whistle in the carriage house when no one else was around. Later on, when she and the other house manager were closing up, she said goodbye to the ghosts and thanked them profusely for making their presence known earlier with the whistle. They were both stunned to hear a disembodied woman's voice say something that sounded like a muffled "you're welcome" in response.

In a world where ghosts are generally thought to be scary things, it is nice to have the merry souls of the Kelton House around to prove otherwise. As exceptional as they were in life, it is no surprise that they are exceptional in death as well.

CHAPTER 4
THE GHOST WHO WASN'T
WESTERVILLE

Do ghosts truly exist, and if so, what exactly are they? People have been mulling over those questions for centuries.

Interest in the subject ran strong after reports came out in 1848 that the Fox sisters of Hydesville, New York, could communicate with spirits. The previous renters of the Foxes' home in Hydesville had problems with mysterious rappings and footsteps. That caused them to vacate the premises after living there for only a year. The Fox family was likewise plagued with the mysterious rappings after they moved in. When Margaret and Kate Fox decided to make a game of it—getting the rappings to follow the pattern of their own claps—they found that the raps would happen on command. They worked out a system to communicate with the unseen force through its rappings. Once the news spread, they had up to five hundred visitors a day coming to check out the phenomena.

A hullabaloo followed. Some people became ardent believers that it was actual communication by spirits, others were equally convinced that it was a hoax and the rest were fascinated whatever the case. Early on, many committees of skeptics were not able to find any earthly explanation for it. Horace Greeley, in mourning over the death of a child, tested the Fox sisters and found them to be credible. The Fox sisters also had some supporters in high places. They were asked by the wife of President Franklin Pierce to do a séance to connect them with the spirit of their deceased son, Benjamin.

Then the movement suffered a blow in the late 1880s when Margaret Fox Kane, one of the Fox sisters, claimed that it had all been a hoax.

There was some speculation that the alcoholic, poverty-stricken Margaret only said that to get vengeance on sister Leah, who had taken financial advantage of the sisters during the height of their popularity. When she recanted a year later, she did cite financial reasons for having made the spurious confession. The confession did not hurt the movement overall, regardless. The Spiritualism religion continued to grow, hitting the peak of its popularity between 1890 and 1920.

Columbus was not immune to the fervor. Columbus physician Dr. J. Everett was so fascinated by the phenomenon that he made repeated trips to Hydesville, New York, to see the Fox sisters work. He later wrote a book about the mystical goings on in the "spirit room" of Jonathan Koons in Athens County. Kate and Margaret Fox saved him one trip by visiting Columbus in 1851. That was a fairly exclusive affair. They did three sittings a day at a private residence on Third Street for which they charged their guests one-dollar admission.

Columbus developed its own celebrity in the world of mediumship. Mrs. Eleanor Martin was a medium in Columbus who, with the help of her spirit friends, specialized in answering questions that were sealed up in envelopes. She was touted as being one of only four mediums in the world who could do this. That claim may have been grossly exaggerated. The practice, called "billet reading," is common among modern Spiritualists. Another local medium, G.C. Walcutt, made paintings of the deceased, again aided by unseen forces. He is said to have made one portrait of a deceased four-year-old in just one hour. The boy's loved ones found it to be so uncannily accurate that it caused them to stand "speechless with wonder and joy." Columbus also gained a reputation among the Spiritualist community through the Light of Truth Publishing Company, which produced books on mediumship and a Spiritualist newspaper.

Rather than being pooh-poohed as just the superstitious leanings of the lower class, Spiritualism was adhered to by many of the movers and shakers of the city. Elizabeth Coit, leader of the women's suffrage movement in Columbus, said, "I have no hesitancy about acknowledging my faith in Spiritualism; and I look upon mediumship as a gift to prize, and not to be ashamed of." Salmon Chase, later to be the secretary of state under Abraham Lincoln, was said to consult mediums while he was in Columbus. There are still three Spiritualist churches in the Columbus area, one right across the street from the site of Chase's old home on State Street.

The newspapermen of the time, however, were less impressed. While they were happy to announce the lectures and demonstrations by various

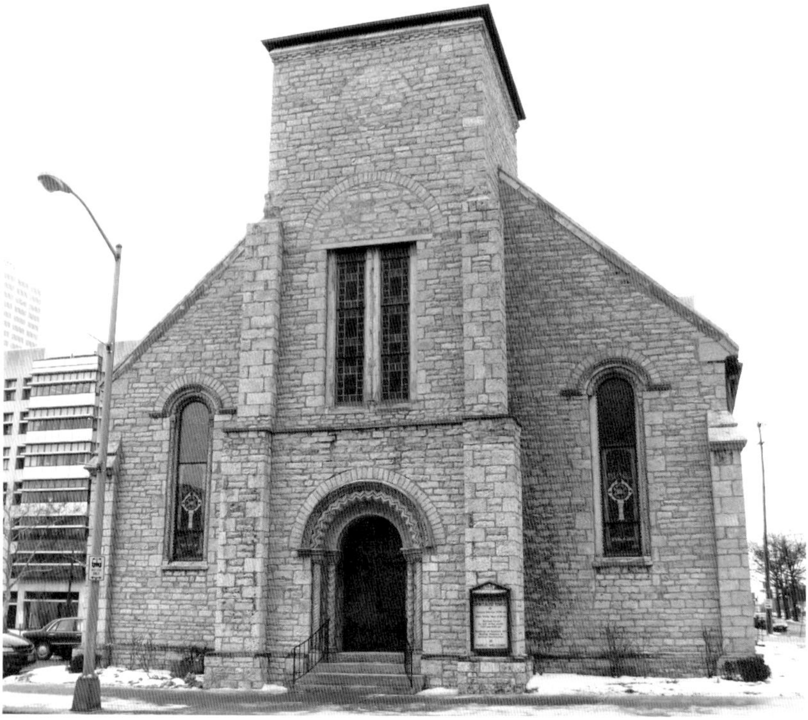

Built in 1902, the First Spiritualist Christian Temple on East State Street is the oldest continuing Spiritualist church in Columbus. *Author's collection.*

Spiritualist mediums that came into town, they were not above mocking them. One particularly humorous article by the fictitious Q.K. Philander Doesticks, P.B., recounts that

> *Months ago I heard mysterious communications tapped out of the dining-table with invisible knuckles, and terrible warnings conveyed by the poker and fire shovel. I became accustomed to that sort of thing, and rather enjoyed a conversation with my bed room furniture. I've passed away many an agreeable hour in talking with my writing desk—enjoyed many a pleasant dialogue with my wash stand.*

Others took a more diabolical view of Spiritualism. They warned their readers of its dangers, linking it with insanity, ill-advised love affairs and suicide.

The newspapermen had some justified concerns about the phenomena. A more balanced account of a Spiritualist lecture and demonstration appeared in the *Ohio State Journal* in 1857. While observing the "ghostly" playing of a drum and tambourine, the reported noted that "the only thing in the way was the darkness. You could hear, but you couldn't see, and everyone knows that 'seeing is believing.' Well, you could not see."

Beyond the fascination with the prospect of being able to communicate with spirits, the Spiritualist movement also raised curiosity about the very nature of ghosts. In her 1850 treatise on the paranormal, *The Night-side of Nature; or, Ghosts and Ghost-seers*, Catherine Crowe considered the mechanics of how and why ghosts usually appear in clothing. Sir William Crookes, a famed British physicist, was one of the first to seriously study psychic phenomena in the 1870s. Mediums were studied as the connection between the living and the dead. They were often viewed more favorably by the scientists than by the newspapermen. Scientific researcher Giuseppi Lapponi made the observation that "the fraudulent practices of some mediums do not prove that all spiritism is fraudulent." Scientific explorations also delved into the physical aspects of how spirits were able to manifest.

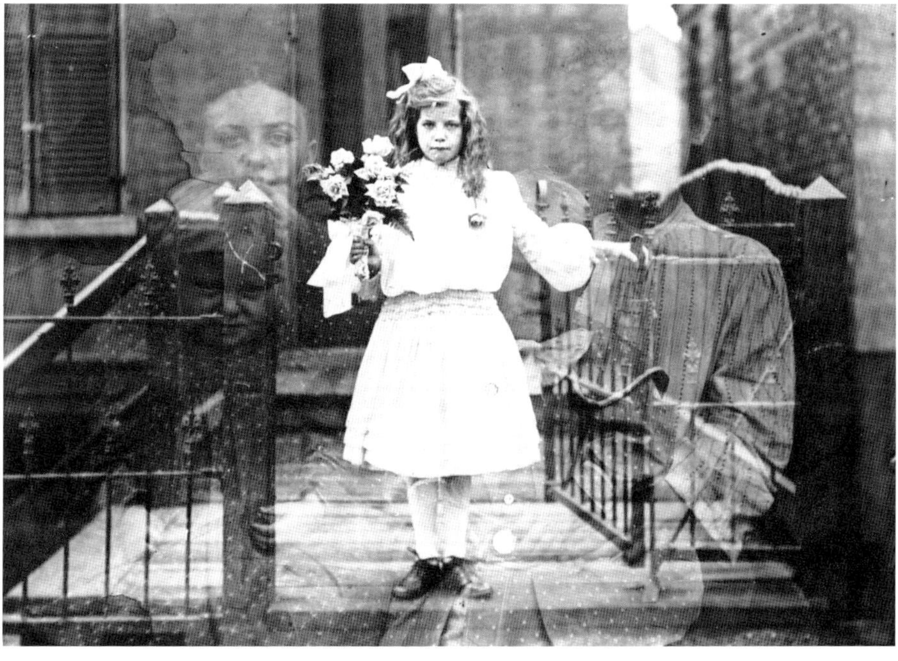

While most Spiritualists were true believers, there were some frauds, as evidenced by this double negative "spirit" photograph from 1905. *Courtesy of the Library of Congress.*

That curiosity continues to this day. With the introduction in 2004 of paranormal research television shows like *Ghost Hunters*, a renewed interest in understanding the hows and whys of ghostly existence sprang up around the nation. There are now over a dozen known groups in Columbus that do paranormal investigations. The current craze puts an emphasis on determining the existence of ghosts through technological devices. Some groups also still use psychic means to try to contact the spirits. Their nineteenth-century predecessors would be proud.

Westerville resident Maggie Cochran (name changed upon request) has some unusual insight into the nature of spirit activity. Back in the 1990s, her doctor put her on beta blocker medication to treat a heart condition. The drug had an interesting effect on her dreams. Instead of having the usual surreal dreams, she started feeling like she was leaving her body overnight. One dream involved going to a Kmart late at night. She observed the stocking clerks getting into a pillow fight. It seemed as real as if she were actually there. One of the pillows burst open and the stuffing flew all over the place. She wasn't a big believer in astral travel, but this dream had her bewildered. "Who would dream about a pillow fight in a Kmart?" she wondered.

Another puzzling dream came close to Christmas. She dreamed that she was back in her hometown, about a two-hour-drive away. She saw a house with a row of doghouses behind it. The dogs started barking at her. The owner of the house came out to try to shush up the dogs. A couple of weeks later, she went down to her hometown to celebrate the holidays with her parents. They decided to take a drive around town to see all of the holiday decorations. Maggie was shocked when they drove by a house that had a row of doghouses in the back, exactly as she had dreamed. She did not remember ever having seen that before.

While the dreams did feel very real, she still wasn't entirely sure that what she had been experiencing were true out-of-body experiences. That changed one night when she dreamed that she went to the drugstore where her husband worked. In the store, she accidentally knocked a bottle of aspirin on the floor. She was surprised that when she tried to pick it up and put it back, her hand seemed to go right through it. The next morning, she told her husband about the dream. He just laughed it off. After all, even normal dreams can be very strange. A few hours later after he had gone into work, she got a call from him. One of his coworkers, who had closed up the previous night, told him something that had him pretty shaken. The coworker was musing about a curious happening. "I sure wish I knew what goes on here at night," she said. "When I locked up this place last night, I had everything cleaned up and in perfect order. However, when I came in this morning, I found a bottle of aspirin on the floor."

When paranormal researchers do ghost investigations, there are a few questions that they inevitably ask of the spirits: "What is your name?" "Do you know that you are dead?" and "Why are you still here?" With living folks like Maggie leaving their bodies in their sleep to engage in nightly escapades, it may be wise for the ghost hunters to add one more question to their repertoire: "Are you on beta blockers?"

CHAPTER 5

POLITICAL HAUNTS

THE SNOWDEN—GRAY HOUSE

Some "ghostly" phenomena can be dismissed as having a natural cause. Perhaps it was just a trick of the light or sound being carried from afar. A door opening by itself could be the result of gravity pulling on unlevel hinges. Rustling sounds in the attic may be the activity of squirrels that found their way in. Other phenomena, however, are harder to explain away. Diane Selby had a brush with the unexplainable when she was a student working at the Kappa Kappa Gamma headquarters in the late 1950s.

She came in one day to hear an odd sound in the closet. She looked in and found the vacuum running. Thinking that the cleaning lady, Adele, had just forgotten to turn it off before putting it away, she flipped the switch off and then went up to her office on the second floor. When Adele came in, Diane mentioned to her that she had left the vacuum running in the closet. Adele gave her a funny look. "That's impossible," she said. "There is no electricity in the closet." Now that Diane thought about it, she hadn't seen the cord coming out of the closet for it to have been plugged in elsewhere. Perplexed, they both went downstairs to investigate. They opened the door to the closet only to find the vacuum cleaner running again.

If having an illustrious history was necessary for a house to be haunted, the Snowden-Gray House would certainly meet the requirement. Prosperous silk merchant Philip T. Snowden and his wife, Abigail, built the elaborate mansion in 1852 just down the block from the Kelton home on Town Street. Abigail was a merchant herself, running her own millinery shop. The Snowdens had a close relationship with famous Civil War–era politician

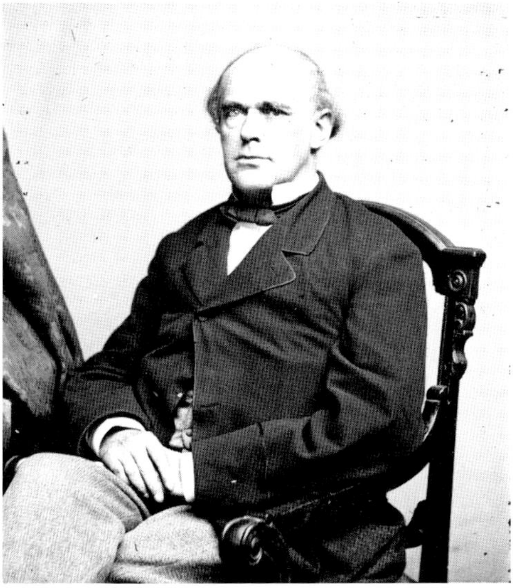

Civil War–era secretary of state Salmon Chase was a frequent visitor to the Snowden mansion while he was governor of Ohio. *Courtesy of the Library of Congress.*

Salmon P. Chase. There are indications that he may have lived with them at some point while he was the governor of Ohio in the 1850s. Unfortunately, Snowden became less prosperous over the years, and his home was sold at a sheriff's auction in 1860. The mansion then became the home of Governor David Tod. During his time there, the home was used to entertain many distinguished guests, including future president Andrew Johnson.

After Tod's tenure as governor ended, the house was bought by banker David S. Gray and his family. The house suffered from a fire in 1872 but was rebuilt under the guidance of renowned architect George Bellows Sr. The Gray family lived there until David Gray's death in 1922. From there, it passed into the hands of the Columbus Women's Club for use as a clubhouse. They added an auditorium onto the back of the building. Financial issues exacerbated by the Great Depression caused them to sell the house less than twenty years later. In the following decade, it passed through many hands, eventually to be used as a boardinghouse.

Like the Kelton House, the Snowden-Gray House was rescued by a women's organization. In 1951, the house was bought by Clara O. Pierce for use as the international headquarters of Kappa Kappa Gamma, a sorority. They restored the façade to the way it had been in the Civil War. Part of the building was turned into the Heritage Museum to honor both the history of the Kappa Kappa Gamma sorority and that of the mansion itself. Now listed on the National Register of Historic Places, the house once again exhibits the grandeur it had in its Victorian heyday.

The vacuum cleaner incident was not the only time that Diane had noticed something odd about the place. An antiques dealer came by once for a tour. Diane was delighted to take him around from room to room while he pointed out the various antiques and told her a little more about them. When she opened the door to one room, however, she was a little

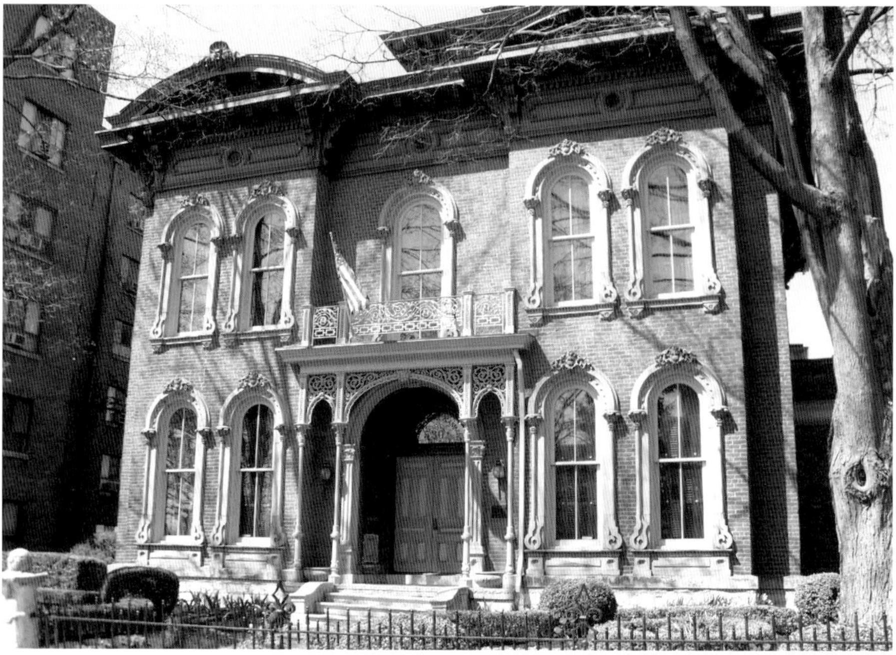

The headquarters of Kappa Kappa Gamma was the home to one of the governors of Ohio during the Civil War. *Author's collection.*

embarrassed to let him in. The room was not as tidy as she would have liked for guests to see. In particular, she noticed that there was an indentation in a love seat, as if someone was sitting in it. She assumed that the stuffing in the upholstery was starting to wear and that Adele had not thought to smooth the indentation when she cleaned the room. She showed him the room quickly and rushed him out as soon as she could. Back out in the hallway, he asked, "Oh, so you felt them, too?" Diane did not know what he meant. He explained that he was psychically sensitive and that he had sensed several spirits in the room. Diane was kind of unnerved by that. The gentleman reassured her that the ghosts weren't there to harm anyone. They just wanted to be left alone. Diane laughed and said that she was more than happy to stay away from them.

The spirits were not as cooperative about leaving her alone. Diane's coworker had a desk right next to the window while Diane's was a little farther over. Just below the window was a courtyard dating back to the years when the house had been the governor's residence. On a pleasant afternoon when they were both working, Diane heard the sounds of a musical quartet playing in the courtyard. The music being played was of a much earlier time. Diane glanced over at her office mate, who did not seem to notice the music at all. Diane was curious about the music. It was too loud to be coming from the neighbors, but this was before transistor radios were commonplace. No one could have had a radio in the courtyard. She got up, looked out the window and saw that the courtyard was mysteriously empty. Wondering if she was losing her mind, she asked her coworker if she heard the music, too. The coworker didn't even look up from what she was doing. She replied that she did hear it. "But," stammered Diane, "there's nobody out there." The coworker, still with her eyes on her work, said, "Yes, I know."

Her coworker was not the only one who was nonchalant about the strange happenings in the house. One day while Diane and her coworker, Karen, were eating lunch downstairs, they saw a man in a black coat going up the stairs. Considering that they were the only staff members in the house at the time and the doors were locked, they were concerned that someone had broken in. They called the police. The police came but were unable to find the man. In fact, they did not find anything amiss. The doors were all locked as they were supposed to have been. Clara Pierce arrived shortly thereafter and in her usual no-nonsense fashion sent the policemen on their way. Diane and Karen told Miss Pierce that they didn't understand why the police didn't find the interloper. They were sure that they had seen a man in black go up the stairs. Miss Pierce was unconcerned. "Yes," she said, very matter-of-factly. "I've seen him before, too."

Other tales over the years have mentioned sightings of a woman in a pink bathrobe and an elegantly dressed woman in a Civil War–era gown. Although Diane has never seen them, she has no doubt that they exist. Whether they lived there when it was a governor's mansion or a run-down boardinghouse, even for ghosts, there's no place like home.

CHAPTER 6
PHANTOMS OF WAR

FRANKLINTON

When John Matthews looked up at the second-story window of his friend's turn-of-the-century house in Franklinton, he was surprised to see a faded Confederate soldier staring back at him. John had some psychic ability, so seeing a ghost was nothing new to him. However, since the house was only about a century old, he could not figure out why a Civil War soldier would be there at all, let alone a Southern one. The answer lay in a little-known facet of Columbus history.

As the capital city of Ohio, Columbus was in a whirlwind of activity during the Civil War. The place was abuzz with politicians and newspapermen debating the righteousness of it. Women showed their support for the soldiers by forming ladies' aid societies, knitting socks and rolling bandages for them. Union soldiers, anxious to join the fray, spent long, tedious hours in training camps being drilled in the arts of war. Their Confederate counterparts spent even longer, more tedious hours in prison camps, waiting for the war to end so that they could go home. Eventually the war did end; the soldiers who survived went back to their civilian lives, and most vestiges of the war were erased by progress. Little remains to remind modern man that the city had ever been affected by the war—except for a few ghosts.

The most famous remnant of the Civil War is the Camp Chase Cemetery, where over two thousand Confederate soldiers are buried. Located on the Hilltop between Broad Street and Sullivant Avenue, Camp Chase had begun life in 1861 as a recruitment center and training camp for Union soldiers. It continued in that capacity throughout the war. However, as changes were made in how the armies dealt with captured enemy soldiers, a new, grimmer role was added. At the beginning of the war, the Union and the Confederacy merely exchanged or paroled captured soldiers, alleviating the need to have long-term facilities to accommodate them. After awhile, the Northern generals realized that it would work to their advantage to deprive the South of having their soldiers return to continue the fight. To accommodate the rising demand for prison space, the southeast section of Camp Chase was pressed into service to house the prisoners.

One of the more unusual groups assigned to guard duty at Camp Chase prison was the Thirty-seventh Iowa Volunteer Infantry. The regiment was comprised of men forty-five years or older, thus giving them the nickname the "Greybeards." They were formed in 1862 to free up regiments of younger, stronger men to do the active fighting. While many of the Thirty-seventh were veterans themselves, with their service going back as far as the War of 1812, they took on the less strenuous responsibilities such as guard duty. Considering that the eldest member of the Greybeards was eighty years old, even guard duty at a prison could be quite challenging. Two of them died while on duty at Camp Chase and were buried in Green Lawn Cemetery.

The original intent was to treat the prisoners at Camp Chase with the respect one would give a fellow soldier. Sentiment against the Confederate prisoners took a sour turn when the locals realized that many of the captured Southerners had brought slaves with them. Rations were cut, and the general care of the prisoners started on a downward spiral at that point. Attitudes toward the Southern prisoners were further aggravated in the summer of 1864 when some of them attempted a jail break. Even though a hospital had been built on the grounds to care for the Confederates, starvation and disease took a heavy toll. Hundreds of the prisoners died every month during the winter of 1864–65.

A hospital built on the site, the Camp Chase Post Hospital, was initially used to serve both Union and Confederate soldiers. The same was true of the two other military hospitals in the area and the Heyl Seminary, a federal prison for women that did double duty as a war hospital. The latter site had previously been used as the Esther Institute, a ritzy school for girls where the daughters of the wealthiest families in the city received their education. As a federal prison, part of the grounds was used to detain female spies from the South in a very genteel and ladylike manner. The hospital section was likewise more pleasant and spacious than most. As demand for hospital space increased, tents were set up around the Heyl Seminary to serve as makeshift wards. Then the Tripler Hospital was built in Franklinton on what is now the corner of North Central and McKinley Avenues.

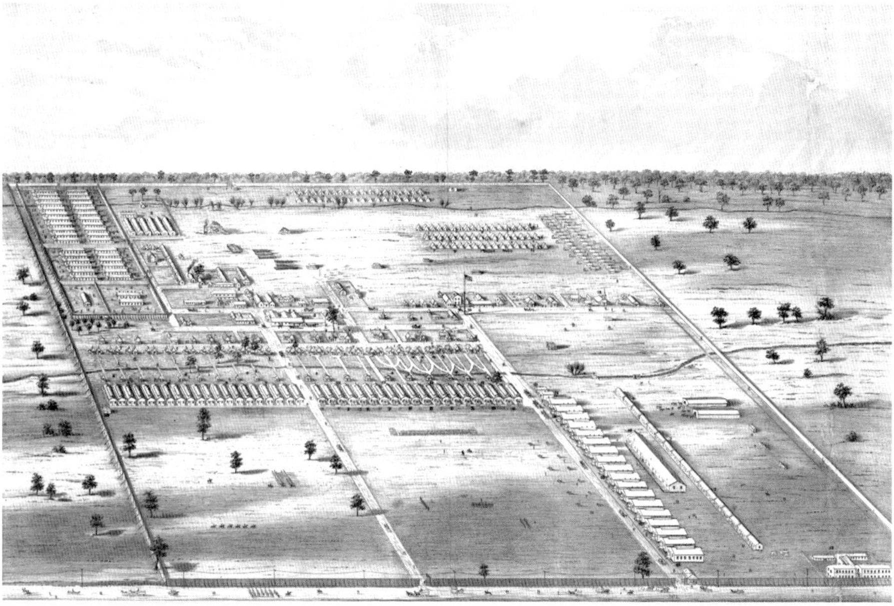

Camp Chase was both a Union training camp and a Confederate prisoner of war camp during the Civil War. *Courtesy of the Library of Congress.*

Over the century following the war, the various sites associated with it were erased by Columbus's continuing drive for modernity. The Heyl Seminary was torn down and replaced by the Columbus Athletic Club. Camp Chase was eventually dismantled, and the land turned into the Westgate housing development. Only the cemetery remains in testimony of the camp's existence. Tripler Hospital continued as a veteran's home for a while. When a national veteran's home was established in Dayton in 1870, the Tripler Hospital became redundant and was closed.

As it turns out, the house that John Matthews (name changed upon request) saw the Confederate soldier in was built on the site of the old Tripler Hospital. The soldiers there have decided not to let their existence be forgotten. Ever since Cheryl York (named changed upon request) and her family moved in, they were beset by an intense amount of ghostly activity. No matter what the season, they could count on at least a couple of paranormal events to occur each day.

The spirits were picky about whom they allowed to live peacefully in their house. Cheryl's sister and her husband had previously rented the house. Doors slamming on their own and other disruptive activity kept them on edge. The final straw for them was when their young daughter was found sleepwalking.

They were frightened by the fact that not only could they not wake her up, but also she was speaking a foreign language. Next, the landlord and his family moved in for a short time. No one knows exactly what went on then, but it was enough to convince them to sell the home in 1985 at a substantial loss, asking for what the land alone was worth. Despite her sister's frightening experiences there, Cheryl York and her husband were more than happy to buy the house.

For Cheryl, the home and its extra roommates turned out to be a good fit. Instead of feeling threatened by the spirits, she found their presence to be welcoming and even calming. The ghosts were not shy about letting her know that they were around. It was common for Cheryl to catch them out of the corner of her eye, feel like she was being touched and hear voices. The Yorks and their friends would also sometimes hear their names being called, only for the other people in the house to say that they had not called them. They would also see dark shadows standing in the doorway of what used to be the back porch or passing by the windows.

Cheryl and her husband were amused when they noticed that their little son, Jason, had an imaginary playmate in his room. Like any sensible parents, they were happy that instead of him believing there was a monster in his closet, he said that his invisible friend lived there. As they had more evidence of other ghostly activity, they came to believe that the imaginary friend was actually a spirit. Years later when they remodeled the house, they found something that added to that impression. In the process of taking the closet apart in order to put in a bathroom, they scraped away the heavy layer of plaster on the closet walls. The wood underneath was heavily scorched. Their theory is that a little boy may have tried hiding in the closet during a house fire and died from smoke inhalation. Jason is now in his early twenties but finds that he can still communicate with the young male spirit.

In addition to the other spirits, Cheryl was pretty sure that her own deceased parents stopped by from time to time. At Christmas, she would set up a little Christmas village that she inherited from her parents. If she ever placed the little houses and villagers in a way that was different from the way her father used to do it, she would come back later and find it corrected.

While most of the house has a warm feel to it, Cheryl was never entirely at ease in her bedroom. Something about the closet felt kind of creepy. That side of the bed also had a strange phenomenon associated with it. Often when she would sit on that side of the bed, she would feel it vibrate. Sometimes the whole bed would shake enough to wake her up at night. When that happened, it felt like a spirit was trying to alert her to something instead of trying to scare her.

The mystery voices were a particular matter of curiosity to the Yorks, since they were a clue to the identity of the spirits. They noticed that the voices sometimes sounded like women and other times like men. They tried making some audio recordings to see if they could capture any electronic voice phenomena, which is having voices turn up in the playback of the recording that had not been heard at the time. In addition to picking up the disembodied voices of a woman and child, they were intrigued to hear a drum being played in a military-style tattoo and a fiddle playing a tune that hearkened back to a time before the Victorian era.

Recently, a medium was brought in to verify that Cheryl wasn't crazy in thinking that the house was haunted. Without any prior knowledge of the house or the activity there, the medium picked up on several things that corresponded with the Yorks' experiences. She felt the presence of two men who had previously owned the land, a woman who had worked there in the Victorian era and the ghost of a little boy who demanded hard candy. Coincidentally, Jason had just offered the young spirit some hard candy a couple of days before. She also confirmed the presence of several Confederate soldiers who had been treated in a hospital on that site. A seriously injured one hung around the closet that bothered Cheryl so much.

One surprise in the medium's visit was that she connected with the spirit of a Revolutionary War soldier who claimed to be one of Franklinton's early settlers. That made sense of the music and drumming that they had heard on their recording. He said that he was buried near a tree in the Franklinton Pioneer Cemetery. Cheryl and the medium went to the cemetery to check on that. The medium was drawn to a spot by a tree in a part of the cemetery where there were no graves marked. The spot she was drawn to corresponded with a place where archaeologists had recently discovered evidence of an unmarked grave.

The dogs in the house likewise noticed the ghostly presences. The family Chihuahua used to bark at them. Now, he remains calm but follows their movement with his eyes. The Shih Tzu has been known to wag his tail at them when Cheryl feels them around. The medium did pick up on one of the previous owners being a man who loved dogs. It makes sense that he would still be befriending them in the afterlife.

In a world where there is so much fear of ghosts, one does not expect the living to coexist peacefully with them. In the case of the Yorks' house, the opposite is true. Over the years, Cheryl has grown so fond of the spirits in her house that she would be loathe for them to leave. The Confederate ghosts may be far from their old homes in the South, but they have found a true home with her.

CHAPTER 7

BOOZE AND SPIRITS

THE JURY ROOM

Columbus is a city that traditionally has not placed much value on preserving its older buildings. Entire streets were destroyed in the 1950s and '60s during construction of new freeways. Old buildings are habitually leveled to make room for more parking lots. One of the more shocking examples of building up only to tear down was the once fashionable City Center Mall. Built just a block away from the statehouse on South High Street, City Center Mall was the chichi place to shop in 1989. Twenty-one short years later, Columbus's experiment in upscale retail had proven to be a dismal failure and was demolished.

Given the "out with the old" attitude Columbus has toward historic preservation, it is a miracle that The Jury Room, Columbus's oldest continuously operating tavern, survived. The exact date of the building's origin is not known, but educated guesses date it to around 1831. It had originally been built as a coach stop to accommodate a variety of clientele. The National Road ran a block north along what is now Main Street, bringing weary travelers to stay overnight in The Jury Room's upper two stories. It was also located near the county courthouse and Brewery District, serving lawyers, judges, businessmen and probably a few felons over the years.

That includes murderers. There was a late-night dispute in 1859 that ended tragically. At a little past midnight on April 1, three young, very drunk German men were standing in front of a "low hovel of ill fame" on the corner of Mound Street and Pearl Alley. One of the men, Paulus Ruprecht, decided that he wanted to partake in their services and knocked on the door. Surprisingly, for a less than respectable business, they kept respectable hours. The owner, Mrs. Frances Miller, informed the young men that the business was closed for the night. She told him to go away. Ruprecht then threatened to kick the door down if he was not given entrance. Mrs. Miller pulled out a gun to warn him off but ended up shooting him when he advanced on her. Oddly, the newspapers demonized Mrs. Miller for being a madam, while overlooking the fact that Ruprecht had threatened a home invasion.

Apparently the illicit side business was doing pretty well during that time period. An addition was built on the back to serve as a bordello in the 1860s. Columbus was a hub of activity during the Civil War, swarming with soldiers, so it makes sense that there may have been an increased market for that kind of business. One story is that Union officers serving at nearby Camp Chase would show their respect for the Confederate officers imprisoned there by bringing them to the bordello for a little rest and relaxation. When a medium visited Camp Chase and asked the spirits there if the story was true, he was given the furtive answer of "top secret!" The rear part of the building once again operated outside the law during Prohibition, when it served as a speakeasy.

It was pretty cheeky of them to be engaging in illegal business, considering that the county jail was right next door. The jail itself could potentially have added to any ghostly activity there. It was sometimes used as an execution yard, such as on December 20, 1858, when Albert Myers was hanged for murder.

The tavern had a very international influence, owned by a string of immigrants and first-generation Americans. Even the gun-happy Mrs. Miller was reported to have a strong foreign accent. John F. Gaiser came to Columbus from Germany in 1865 and ran the place from the 1870s into the early 1890s. In the mid-1880s, it was listed as a boardinghouse as well as a saloon. By 1890, the tavern was a little more upscale, at least in print. It was listed in the city directory as the Wine and Beer Hall, featuring "fine liquors and cigars." Peter Weirich and Son took over for several years until Frenchman Emil Hess bought the tavern. He owned it for another decade or so. Continuing the upscale trend, Christian Welde from Germany bought it and renamed it the Cafe. He lived and worked there and eventually even died there of cancer in 1928.

The business changed hands not infrequently for most of the next six decades. The big exception was during the 1940s through most of the 1950s, when it was run by Irvin Howerton and later by Harry McKay as Irvin's

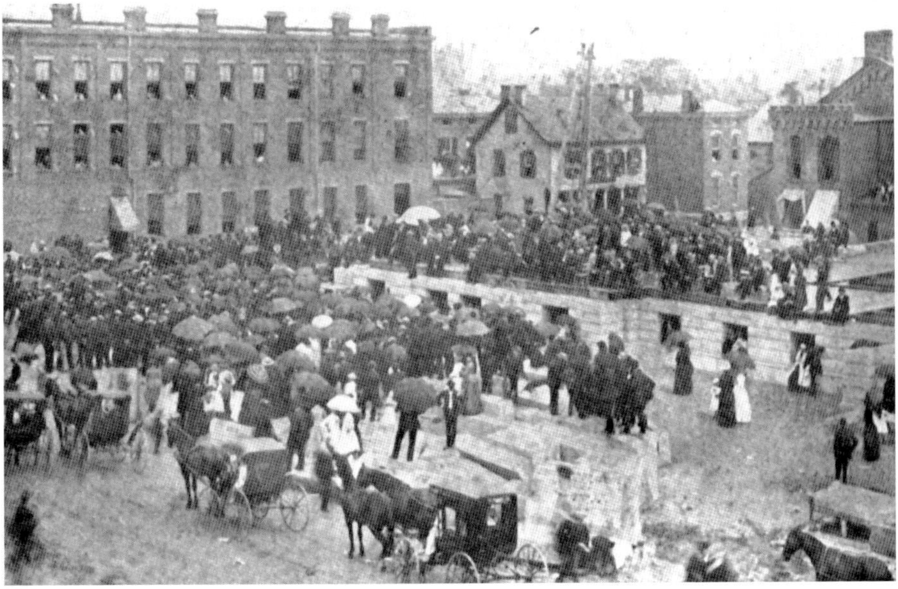

The Jury Room can be seen in the background of the construction of the Franklin County Courthouse in 1885. *Courtesy of Columbus Metropolitan Library.*

Place. Throughout that time, it kept a reputation as being a neighborhood gathering place.

With all that history behind it, Georgia Byrd and her husband, Dave, were the perfect guardians for the building. As real estate appraisers, they had developed a deep love of old buildings. When they had the opportunity to rent office space in the back of the building in the 1980s, they jumped at the chance. They renovated it, keeping a reverence for the building's age. Eventually, they became its sole owners.

Georgia did not take it too seriously when the old-timers at the bar told her that strange and ghostly occurrences took place there. It was easy enough to assume their tales were born of too much drink or a desire to pull her leg. After all, she had been working in the other part of the building for years without any experiences she could consider paranormal. It didn't take long, though, for her to find out that the old-timers were telling the truth.

The spirits are particularly active during renovations. One of the oddest events happened when a workman had come in to fix a broken dumbwaiter after hours. He went upstairs to the second floor and started working on it from up there. When he turned around, instead of seeing the office that the room normally contained, he was greeted by a scene from long ago. He

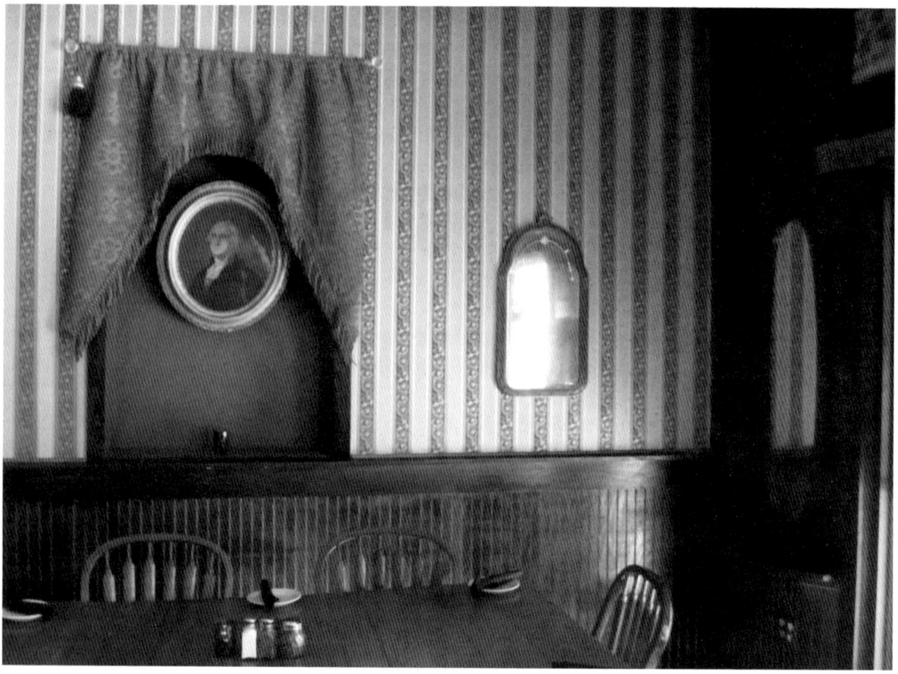

The Jury Room has been renovated to make it look like it might have when it first opened in 1831. *Author's collection.*

found himself in a kitchen, as the room had been in its early years, where a woman from ages past was contentedly cooking. After that, he refused to work there after hours.

The ghosts appreciate a warm fire. There have been times when an employee has come in to find a cheery fire in the gas fireplace. Intriguingly, there was no fire on when the place had shut down the previous night. Georgia had trouble figuring out how this could have happened. The fireplace had been put in by the previous owners. Although it was fairly new, it was awkward to turn on, requiring two hands. There was no way for it to have accidentally turned on by itself.

The spirits also have an ornery sense of humor. As with any bar, glasses get broken from time to time. Georgia wisely kept a spare case of glasses in the basement. When she was running low on glasses, she went down to the cellar to retrieve the spares. She looked where she thought she had put them, but they were not there. She then looked all over the basement, moving other boxes to and fro to figure out where the glasses had gone. It proved a fruitless task. She finally gave up and went out to buy more. When she got back, she brought one of the new cases down to store in the basement. There—right where she had looked originally—was the case of glasses she had been looking for.

The Byrds still own the building, but they sold the bar business to Elizabeth Lessner in 2010. That turned out to be another good match. The ghosts should appreciate her respect for the history of the place. She retained the name of The Jury Room in keeping with tradition. An even nicer tip of the hat was that she had the place restored to look like it did when it was a coach stop 180 years ago, complete with period furniture. While the workers there have not reported any new activity since the business changed hands, the staff remains hopeful that the spirits will come out to play or maybe just have a drink.

CHAPTER 8

ON THE RIVER'S EDGE

DUBLIN

On June 1, 1810, John Sells, the founder of Dublin, Ohio, stood near the eastern bank of the Scioto River and beheld a horrifying scene. A gray-haired Wyandot chief in his finest clothes knelt at the edge of a shallow grave and prayed. As soon as he was finished, a warrior drew a tomahawk and smashed the old man in the head. While the chief lay there in agony, another warrior pointed to some drops of sweat on the dying man and gleefully proclaimed that it was proof of the old man's guilt. The first warrior came back up and dealt a few more hard blows. With that, John Sells witnessed the death of his friend, Chief Leatherlips.

The history behind Leatherlips's death goes back decades beforehand and affected entire nations of indigenous people. The crux of the matter was land ownership. In the late 1700s and early 1800s, tensions ran high between the Native Americans who lived in Ohio and the white settlers who claimed the land as their own.

Indigenous peoples had lived in the area for millennia. Remnants of the early inhabitants could be seen in the hundreds of mounds and earthworks that dotted the land, dating back 2,500 to 3,000 years. In the sixteenth century, the Mound Builder cultures faded away from the territory, replaced by newer groups. The Iroquois Confederacy migrated in from their base in central New York, only to move back a few generations later to protect their original homeland from French and English interlopers. The Shawnee, Wyandot, Delaware and Mingo tribes had all flowed into the central Ohio area in their wake.

At first, the native peoples only had to deal with the occasional French trapper or missionary passing through the area. That soon changed. By the mid-1700s, territorial disputes were flaring up between the French and the English. The Virginia Land Company claimed land in the Ohio Valley, as did the French. Christopher Gist, an emissary of the Virginia Land Company, signed a treaty with the Miami chief called Old Britain in Pickawillany, now known as Piqua. The French were enraged that the Miamis continued to trade with the British despite French orders not to. In 1752, the French retaliated by sending a force of Frenchmen and their Indian allies to attack the Miami. Old Britain and over a dozen other Miamis were killed. Meanwhile, the territorial dispute between the French and the British intensified over the next two years, culminating in the French and Indian War. The English won, and the French relinquished their claim to the area.

Not all of the native tribes that fought on the French side were willing to accept the English as the new owners of their land. Before the war even ended, Ottawa chief Pontiac assembled a force from several tribes and commanded assaults against British forts and settlements. One of the assaults was on the future site of Columbus, killing a Pennsylvania trader named Matthew McCrea. Pontiac's forces were unable to capture either of two strategic sites, Fort Detroit and Fort Pitt, where Pittsburg is today. Without these major forts under their control, they had no hope of success. Their efforts were further undermined when Lord Jeffrey Amherst, a British commander, had smallpox-infected blankets sent to the native forces. The rebellion petered out.

The British tried to keep the peace by banning settlement to the north and west of the Ohio River. Some colonists ignored the ban, leading to horrifying actions on their part. In 1774, settlers murdered the family of Mingo chief Logan. He began another rebellion. Not long after, Colonel William Crawford led an attack on a Mingo camp, where Columbus now stands. The men of the camp were away hunting. Crawford's forces killed several women, children and old men and burned the camp to the ground. Crawford was eventually caught by the Delaware and burned to death near Upper Sandusky.

The Revolutionary War years were marked by attacks by the native peoples against white settlements and retaliatory strikes by the colonial armies against native settlements. For the most part, the strife occurred in the northern and western parts of Ohio, leaving central Ohio to relative peace. However, the Revolutionary War posed a new problem for the indigenous peoples after it ended. The cash-poor Continental Congress decided to pay off the veterans for their service in the war with land in the Northwest Territories, including the land of Ohio. The Ordinance of 1787 set up a system for governing the Northwest Territories and set the stage for settlement by the colonials.

In 1790, Josiah Harmar was sent on a mission to take an army northward through western Ohio to clear out the natives. He met with a distinct lack of success. In 1791, Arthur St. Clair, governor general of the Northwest Territories, followed suit. He failed even more miserably, with nearly one thousand soldiers and their families being killed at the Battle of the Wabash. His adversaries were led by Miami chief Little Turtle and Blue Jacket of the Shawnees, both of whom were brilliant military tacticians.

George Washington assigned General Anthony Wayne to try again a few years later. This time, the American army succeeded. A surprisingly short battle, lasting less than an hour, took place at Fallen Timbers near Toledo, giving "Mad Anthony" Wayne a decisive win. Leaders of the opposing nations signed a treaty at Fort Greenville to end the conflict. It gave the southern two-thirds of Ohio over to American settlement, while allowing the native populations to stay in the northern third. Leatherlips was one of the Indian leaders who signed the treaty.

Chief Leatherlips believed in finding a peaceful solution to the conflict. Over the next several years, he befriended the white settlers in the area that was to become Dublin. This did not sit well with other Native American leaders such as Shawnee chief Tecumseh and his brother "The Prophet," Tenskwatawa, who were against the Treaty of Greenville to begin with.

After another tribe member and his horse died of illness, Leatherlips was accused of having caused the deaths. He was placed on trial for witchcraft. The white settlers believed these to be trumped-up charges ordered by Tecumseh and The Prophet in order to get a man whom they considered to be a traitor out of the way. Several white settlers were in attendance at the trial, hoping to prevent a travesty of justice. John Sells was among them. He tried to trade a fine horse for Leatherlips's freedom. It was to no avail.

Leatherlips may be long dead, but his name still lives on in the folklore of Dublin. In more recent years, a rather condescending claim has cropped up regarding his ghost. The story is that the rain that falls on the Memorial Tournament in Dublin every year is the result of a curse by Leatherlips in revenge for his untimely death. It seems unlikely that a man who gave his life in the interest of peace would be concerned about disrupting a golf

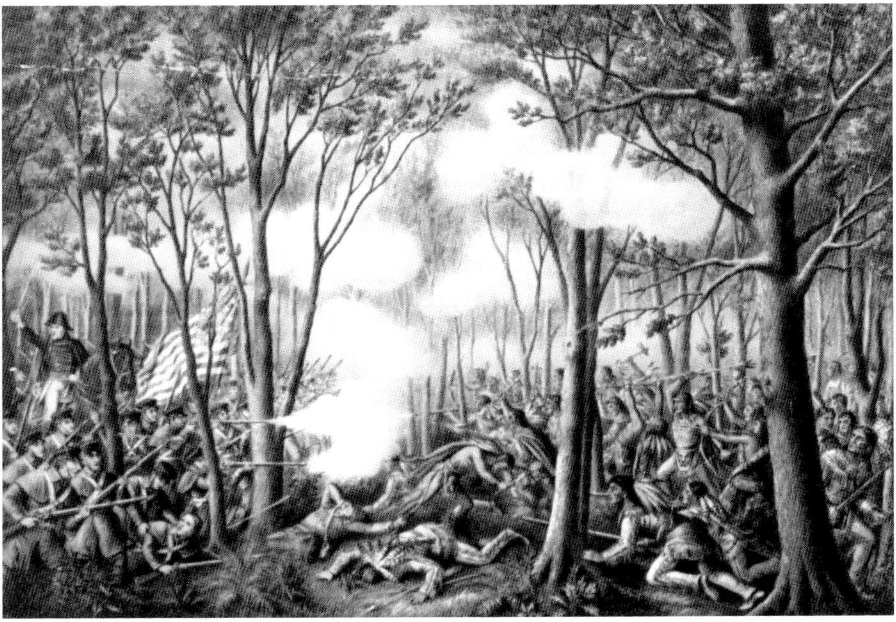

Shawnee chief Tecumseh, who may have ordered the execution of Leatherlips, was later killed at the Battle of Tippecanoe. *Courtesy of the Library of Congress.*

tournament. However, old-timers in the area are familiar with an earlier, more plausible legend. The traditional tale was that every year on the anniversary of his death, Leatherlips's spirit had been seen rising from his grave. He is said to walk down to the banks of the Scioto where his village once stood, mourning the violence that affected both the natives and the settlers in the quest to control the land.

CHAPTER 9

THE SOULS OF HOSPITALITY

HARRISON HOUSE BED & BREAKFAST

"Is this house haunted?" That is a question that Lynn Varney has gotten used to hearing from the guests at her Harrison House Bed & Breakfast the moment they walk in the door.

Lynn knew that there was something different about the house from the beginning. It was a fluke that she had even come here to begin with. Her plan had been to move out of Columbus where she had lived for many years to start a bed-and-breakfast somewhere in northern Ohio, closer to Lake Erie. However, her real estate agent suggested that she might want to take a look at a house in Victorian Village. He warned her that the sellers would only sell it to the "right" person. Lynn had no interest in Victorian houses or in staying in Columbus, but she decided to humor the real estate agent by looking at it. Much to her surprise, as soon as she set foot on the front steps, she knew that she had to have the house. That feeling increased once she walked inside. Remembering the real estate agent's warning, she started to worry that the owners would not consider her to be the right person to buy it. Luckily, that was not the case.

If anything, the house seemed to have chosen her. There were some odd coincidences that made her feel even more like she was in the right place. After she moved in, she found a George Carruth water bowl in the garden in the shape of a cat. That particular design was one of Carruth's more uncommon pieces. It also happened to be the same as one she already owned. Down in the basement, there was a wood cutout of Santa Claus, the same as one that Lynn used to own. That type of item was sold only for one

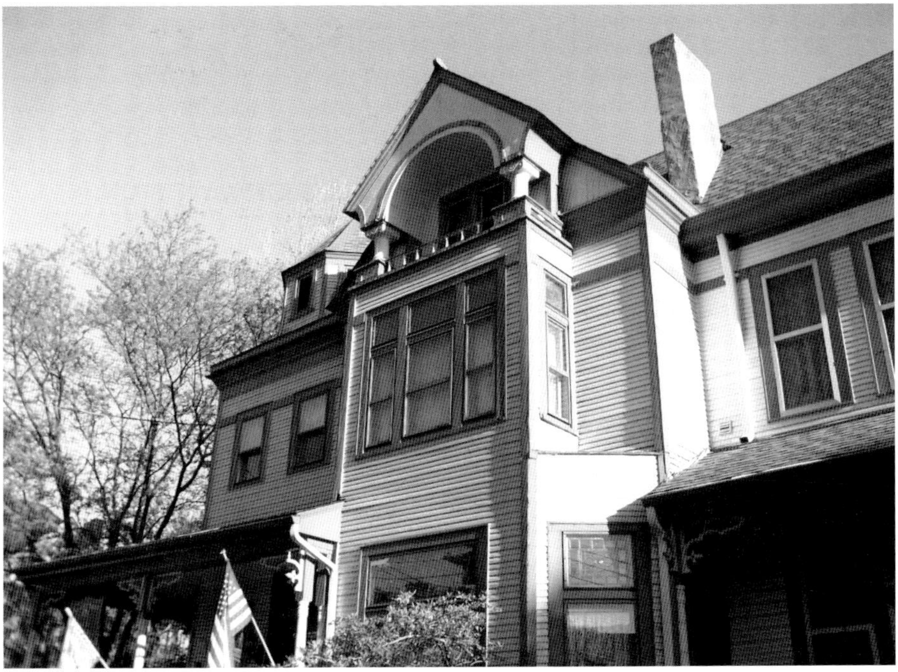

The Harrison House Bed & Breakfast is an exuberant example of the architectural styles found in Victorian Village. *Author's collection.*

year by the Children's Hospital Twig organization as part of their annual fundraiser. The chances of finding another one in the house she had just bought were astronomically low.

After Lynn had been there for a couple of weeks, she started to notice some things that didn't make sense. Her first clue that the house might be haunted came when she found an indentation in a bed on the second floor, as if someone had been sitting on it. There were no guests in the house, and she knew that she hadn't made it. She smoothed it out, only to come back later and find the indentation there again. She had a strong sense that another woman was in the room.

Then little things like paper clips started disappearing. She kept a binder clip on her reservation book, which disappeared, only to show up later. Next, a check that a guest had left in payment disappeared for a week. She knew darn well that she had received the check, but it was nowhere to be found. It reappeared a week later in one of the places where she had already looked.

Not content with such a small audience, the spirits decided to start making themselves known to the guests. Lynn has a routine of getting breakfast prepared and then sitting and doing the crossword puzzle before getting back to breakfast. The paper and pen end up sitting on the countertop for an hour or two while Lynn takes care of her guests. One morning, as they were finishing breakfast, a guest casually asked if she had any spirits in the house. Lynn admitted that yes, she thought so. As she was saying that, the pen rolled off the countertop, even though it had been sitting stationary for an hour or so.

She also started getting clues that there wasn't just one spirit there. One day while she was up in the attic room cleaning, she found a toy soldier in the ceiling light. Lynn threw it away, thinking that the old housekeeper just didn't do a very good job. She completely forgot about it until months later when a young couple staying in the room asked her where the soldier was. They were quite distressed. They explained that it was a guardian for the room and made a little cork man to replace the soldier. Half a year later, another couple asked about the soldier and said the same thing. They brought a new toy soldier the next year. Since then, others have left all sorts of soldiers, tanks and more. The toy soldier seemed to be attached to the spirit of a young teenage boy. Over time, more and more guests mentioned sensing him. Belief in the young male spirit strengthened when a guest, himself a teenage boy, reported actually seeing him. To add to the mystery of the house's normally invisible occupants, the young man also saw an adult man in the bathroom door as plain as day. The teenager got the impression that the male spirit looked after the boy, although the man was from a later time period.

Even more clues surfaced to alert Lynn of her extra housemates. She would smell phantom smells on occasion, usually of faint cigars or cigarettes. Earlier on, though, the spirits announced themselves in a distinctly unpleasant manner. Lynn was up on the stairwell one day when she smelled a strong, terrible rotting odor. She wasn't sure what would have caused it, but she went downstairs to get some air freshener to try to get rid of the smell. By the time she had gotten back to the stairs, the smell was gone. The smell had been so strong just a minute or two earlier that it didn't make sense that it would have disappeared so quickly. She went upstairs and smelled the odor again, although this time it was a little fainter. The smell moved down the hallway, growing fainter until it disappeared altogether. Lynn was understandably disturbed by this. She was used to spirits being around by this point, but having the smell of rotting flesh in the house was bad for business! Thankfully, the spirit realized this and learned to tone down his odor to just that of the cigarettes. This spirit enjoys the company of the living. He uses the faint scent of cigarettes to let them know that he is there.

In addition to the phantom smells, the spirits would sometimes make their presence known through more physical means. There is a big, heavy picture at the end of the hallway. Despite being securely hung, it would often be found on the floor face down. This tended to occur during times when the activity in the house was the highest.

Just as the house drew Lynn to it, it also drew the occasional psychic. Not long after the teenager saw the spirits, a woman stayed there who was a medium. She asked to go to the room where other guests had reported feeling the spirits the most strongly. Without knowing any more about it, she and her husband went up there for a half hour. She came back down and said that there was a woman who was either the matriarch of the house or had been a head housekeeper there. That spirit was the one who had brought Lynn to the house and chosen her to be its next owner. The lady went on to say that the spirit woman had a very clear message that she wanted to have passed on to Lynn. It was: "She likes you very much, and she is very happy with what you are doing here." The medium told Lynn to remember that. Then she went on to describe a young boy about thirteen or fourteen who had been injured in the street and brought back to die here. She said,

> *When he was alive, the attic was his play space, and he liked to play with toy soldiers. He isn't very aware of people in the present time. There is also a man from a later time who looks after him. This man was a boarder who smoked. He died in the house from some kind of lung disease. She smelled him before she was otherwise aware of him because he had a strong odor of smoke and rotting flesh. There is another man who is either schizophrenic or bipolar who also died in the house. He is harmless, but he can get quite agitated. When that happens, he runs through the house and knocks things off the walls.*

Within a month, another couple came to stay. As soon as the woman walked in, she said, "Oh, you have spirits here." When questioned about that, she said that she was aware of them because they were very strong spirits. While Lynn was giving them a tour of the house, the guest stopped on the second floor landing and said, "By the way, there is someone here who likes you very much and is very happy with what you are doing here." Lynn was astounded. The guest mentioned that she felt like there was a portal on the stairwell and up on the third floor. She said that she sensed a woman who was the matriarch of the house, a boy who played up in the attic, a man who smells really horrible who looks after the boy, and another man who was bipolar or schizophrenic. Lynn had not told her any of this.

Lynn herself has never seen the spirits except out of the corners of her eyes. However, she does hear them a lot. They open and shut the doors frequently, as if they can't go through the doors otherwise, and footsteps are also frequently heard when there is no one else in the house. She has heard them speak as well. She was downstairs cooking breakfast one morning when she heard someone say, "Good morning, Lynn!" She said good morning in return and looked up to greet what she thought was her guest. There was no one standing there. She looked around the first floor, but she was the only one there.

The spirits are more than happy to interact with the guests, as a bunch of friends found out. After hearing some of the tales on a ghost tour, the group decided that it would be fun to spend the night there to see if they might have their own paranormal experiences. One of them got more than she had bargained for.

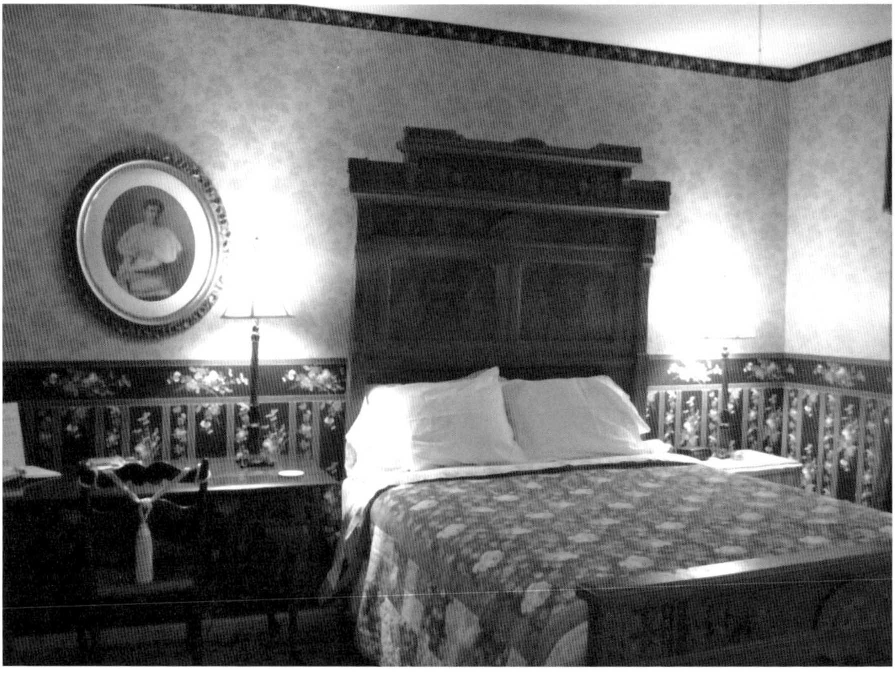

A portal to the other world is said to exist near the door to this room in the Harrison House Bed & Breakfast. *Author's collection.*

As the friends were sitting around the dining room table on the night of their sleepover, the subject of finding a ghost in one's bed came up in the conversation. The single women in the group all started laughing and teasing each other about who was going to have a spectral bedmate come snuggle up with them in the middle of the night. They laughed even harder when it was pointed out that in order to accommodate the large size of the group, most of them were already sharing a bed with someone. Jennifer Parsons (name changed on request), the most outgoing of the group, was jokingly voted by the women as the one who should have a ghostly late-night visitor. As it happened, she was staying in room three, one of the most haunted rooms in the house.

The next morning, the guests began comparing notes about anything paranormal that had happened the night before. Jennifer asked if anyone else had heard the loud caterwauling coming from within the house that had awoken her at dawn. She was bewildered to find that no one else had heard it. She said that things got stranger from there. Once awake, she felt someone nudging her over closer and closer to the edge of the bed. She assumed that her bedmate was just being a bed hog. When she looked at her friend to tell her to move back over, she was shocked to find a man lying between them. He was lying on top of the covers, fully clothed, complete with a hat, shoes and overcoat. He seemed to be pleased with himself for taking part in the women's joke from the previous night. He laid there, looking up at Jennifer with an impish little smile on his face. Jennifer, however, was not likewise amused. She frantically started thinking, "Please go away, please go away, please go away!" With that, he sat up and got off the bed. He walked a few steps and then faded away.

While it isn't easy, the spirits are also happy to try to communicate with the guests. A guest brought in a Ouija board, through which they have been trying from time to time to talk with the souls. They have repeatedly gotten the names Moby for the boy, Cedric for the smoking man and Jakob for the other man. During one session, a closet door opened by itself. Attempts to record the Ouija board sessions have never panned out, though. Even though the people doing the recordings had been careful to check the recorders during the sessions, on playback the recordings were garbled or had disappeared altogether.

The Ouija board sessions are a source of curiosity, answering some questions while raising others. While the historic records do not show anyone having lived there with the names that came up in the Ouija board sessions, there is a curious similarity between Cedric and a man who had lived there for several years in the 1940s. The man, who had owned a Greek restaurant in downtown Columbus, died of gangrene of the stomach. Gangrene causes one's flesh to rot. Another occupant in the early 1920s also died of gangrene.

Figuring out just who the spirits are has proven to be a challenge. One person you might expect to haunt the house is the first owner, who seemed to have a deep connection to the place. The house was built in 1890 by Amos J. Solomon, a banker and architect. The house was originally facing Harrison Avenue, but he later added a new front to the side of the house to give it a more prestigious Fifth Avenue address. Solomon then moved out of Franklin County to pursue a career opportunity. That turned out to be a flop. Newspaper reports from 1910 indicate that a bank he had been in charge of was so poorly managed that it had to close. Solomon could not stay away from his house, however. By 1920, he was divorced and back living in the house, this time as a lodger. By 1925, he was once again married and listed as the head of the household.

The house did have some fairly well-known owners. In the early 1930s, the house was owned by the Zanetos family. The family name may not be familiar to modern folks, but the name of their business, the Anthony Thomas Candy Company, probably is. Olentangy Management Company, a subsidiary of Battelle Memorial Institute, bought and renovated the place in 1965. This was part of their plans to rejuvenate the neighborhood, which had fallen into a sorry state since its peak in the late Victorian era. Cardinal Industries brought it back to its former glory further when they took it over in 1980. They did more renovations and made some changes to the structure to use it as a corporate retreat.

While the owners before Lynn didn't notice any haunting activity, one has to wonder if the other early owners weren't already aware of the spirits there. Between 1916 to 1925 the house changed hands on almost a yearly basis, despite being relatively new. To add to the mystery, one of the owners in the late 1920s sold the house only to move into the house next door.

Why do the spirits linger there? Cedric gave his answer during one session with the Ouija board. The reason is actually quite simple: "You can't smoke in heaven!"

CHAPTER 10

Murder, Mayhem and Manifestations

The Ohio State University Neighborhoods

Over the years, most students who lived in the neighborhoods immediately surrounding the campus have told stories about how freaky their apartments were. There may be more to their complaints than just aggravating roommates and neglectful landlords. Some of the most seemingly innocuous buildings in the area have frightening pasts.

One of the more surprising stories occurred close to where St. Stephen's Episcopal Church stands today. Looking at that hall of spirituality and fellowship, one would hardly expect that its grounds had been the site of a homicide and suicide in 1909. In that year, a couple named William and Clare Puryear was living in a house at 22 West Woodruff Avenue. The couple had only been married for a year, and to their neighbors looked to be perfectly happy. However, there was a dark side to their marriage.

William Puryear, an electrical engineer and machinist at The Ohio State University, was known for his bad temper. On the morning of June 22, he accused his wife of infidelity with some unknown man and struck her. After he left, Clare Puryear's brother, Fred West, came over. She told him about the fight. He was so concerned about the violence against his sister that he went to his house, got a gun and came back to protect her. When William Puryear returned, he likewise came back armed. He pulled a gun on the siblings, killing West and seriously wounding his wife. By the time the police arrived, Puryear had written a suicide note, blaming West and his wife for

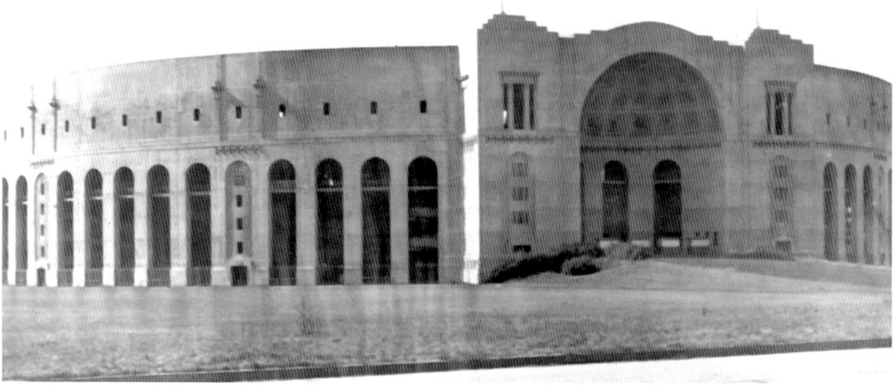

The Ohio Stadium was originally planned to be built across the street from the site of a brutal murder. *Courtesy of Ohio Historical Society.*

the shootings. He also set fire to the house. Not content with the destruction he had already caused, he shot at the police before killing himself.

Eight years later, when plans were being made to build Ohio Stadium, the original thought was to put it where Ramseyer Hall is now, across the street from the murder site. University president William Oxley Thompson did not like the idea of the stadium being on what was geographically the highest point on campus, thus elevating it over the academics. In deference to him, the decision was made to place it west of the campus instead. One has to wonder if the memory of that blood-soaked day, still fresh in their minds, did not also play into the decision. Haunted or not, holding tailgates on the site of violent, brutal deaths would seem a bit disrespectful.

However, having a murder on the site is no guarantee of a place being haunted nor is it a requisite. Peculiar happenings can occur in places where no one ever died. One seemingly mundane house in the campus area had phenomena that were bizarre even for a haunting.

Sue Gall should have known there was something up with the rooming house from the moment the landlady opened the door. It was September 1971; classes at The Ohio State University were due to start in two weeks. Sue had just moved to Columbus and was dismayed to find that all of the apartments in the area had already been rented. It seemed a stroke of luck when she found the ad in the paper for rooms at a house on West Tenth Avenue, just on the edge of campus. She wasn't as sure when she saw the landlady. The woman who greeted her at the door was a disheveled elderly lady with hair like a rat's nest. She showed Sue around the various rooms, proudly pointing out that she had redecorated them herself recently. Sue found the drawings on the wall on the ugly side and was likewise unsettled by the fact that none of the rooms had been rented out yet. However, she liked the atmosphere of the third-floor bedroom and decided to take it.

Just a week later, strange things started happening. She returned home in the wee hours of the morning after working her shift at Plank's Restaurant. It had been a long night, and she had driven home in pouring rain. She climbed the stairs to make a pit stop at the restroom on the second floor, the only one available to the boarders, and was dismayed to find it locked. She was also surprised, considering that she was still the only boarder at that point. She then went up to her room, only for the key to break off in the lock. Exasperated, she went down and woke up the landlady to report that she could not get into her room. The landlady quickly threw a housecoat over her nightgown and came out to help. On the way up the stairs, Sue mentioned to the landlady about the bathroom door being locked as well. The landlady was stunned, saying that the bathroom didn't even have a lock on it!

The landlady let Sue into an unused apartment on the third floor to use the restroom there while she went to work on the jammed lock on her room. When Sue came back out just a couple of minutes later, she was again surprised to see the landlady, now fully dressed, coming out of the second-floor bathroom door. "How did you do that?" Sue asked. "Oh," the landlady explained, "I just climbed up on the neighbor's roof, sidled over to the bathroom window, opened it and opened the door from the inside." Sue was incredulous that she could possibly have gotten dressed and done all that in just the couple of minutes it had taken Sue to use the restroom. Even more perplexing was that the landlady was still bone dry despite the heavy rain outside. She had also somehow managed in that short period of time to have fixed the lock to Sue's room.

Over the next week, the boardinghouse quickly filled up with tenants, who, like Sue, found themselves with little choice, as autumn quarter classes were about to begin. One of her coworkers at Plank's was among them. From there, more odd things happened.

A trash can was kept in the hallway of the second floor where most of the rooms were. Sue came home one day to find the trash from it strewn all over the floor, up and down the length of the hallway. None of the tenants would own up to having done that. From what Sue had seen of their characters, none of them seemed like they would have done it either as a joke or to be obnoxious.

Things became more disturbing weeks later. She was woken out of her sleep in the middle of the night by the sound of her door opening. She hadn't heard a key in the lock, even though she had always kept the door locked. She was instantly wide awake, adrenaline pumping through her. Unsure how to handle the situation, she feigned being asleep. She could feel a strong presence coming near her until it was standing over her. The sound of its breathing filled her with terror. Then, as suddenly as it had come, the presence disappeared. Sue got up and checked the door. It was still locked. Then she realized that when the presence disappeared, she did not hear the door open again for it to have left through.

As if that weren't enough, Sue discovered that the landlady had some slovenly housekeeping habits. She hadn't been overly concerned about the possibility of ghosts in the house, but the possibility of cockroaches was another matter. She moved out for good as soon as the quarter was over.

It is hard to say what was behind the mysterious goings on at the rooming house. The answer may have to do with the family that lived there in the first half of the twentieth century. A series of deaths hit the family in the 1930s. First, an elderly man died of heart troubles in 1934. There is nothing unusual about that. However, his wife died three years after that from a fall in the house. Their son inherited the house, only to die three years later as well. All of them died in a nearby hospital instead of in the house. Still, with so many deaths in the family in a short time, it would not be surprising if at least one of them decided that it wasn't their time to go.

There may be certain advantages to having a ghostly roommate instead of a living one. Chances are that they don't bring home one-night stands or leave "science experiments" growing in the refrigerator. On the minus side, they can be just as loud and annoying. When in doubt, opt for a living one. They are more likely to pay their share of the rent.

CHAPTER 11

STAGE FRIGHT

PALACE THEATRE

Late one evening in a darkened theater, a small group of people sat around a table trying to talk to the dead. Ostensibly, they were part of a private party celebrating the grand reopening of the Palace Theatre, one of the few remaining gems from the golden era of theaters in Columbus. The guest of honor was Harry Blackstone Jr. Blackstone was a popular magician who had performed at the Palace, as had his famous father, Blackstone the Magician, decades before. According to legend, the organizers thought it might be fun to hold a séance to contact Howard Thurston, the rival of Blackstone's father.

Columbus native Thurston had likewise performed in the Palace Theatre in the early decades of the twentieth century. His showmanship, along with his bevy of beautiful and scantily clad assistants, kept generations of theatergoers spellbound. While he is not well known in modern times, he was one of the premier magicians of his day. Many magic historians consider him to be the greatest magician of all time, eclipsing even Harry Houdini. He no doubt had proved a worthy rival to Blackstone.

Thurston was an odd choice for a séance, though, given his track record. Before he died in 1936, he had made a pact with his friend, Claude T. Noble. The deal was that if Noble visited his crypt at Green Lawn Abbey on the anniversary of his death, Thurston would manifest proof of his existence in the spirit world. After seven years of trying with no success, any belief that Noble may have had in ghosts was shattered. When asked about his failure to contact Thurston, he commented that the money spent on spiritualism every year would be better spent on war bonds.

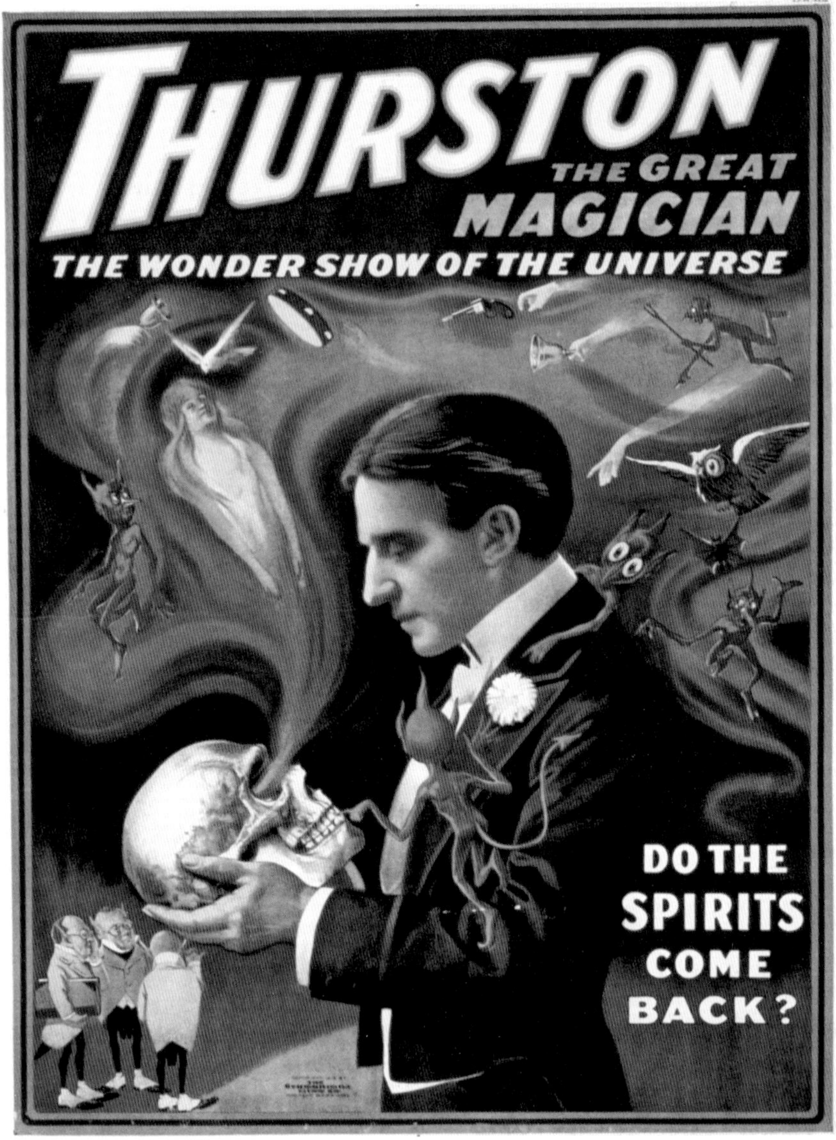

Columbus native Howard Thurston was thought by many to be a better magician than Houdini. *Courtesy of the Library of Congress.*

Under the circumstances, it should not have been a surprise that the séance at the Palace Theatre did not go as planned. When the medium made contact, one side of her face sagged, and she had difficulty speaking, as if she were a stroke victim. The séance party became excited. Thurston's official cause of death was pneumonia, but he had suffered a severe stroke a couple of weeks before he died. Could they have actually managed to contact him? Their excitement turned to concern when the spirit indicated that he had been murdered in the theater. They were not able to get any clearer information out of him. The spirit's identity remains a mystery to this day. There are no reports of a death ever having taken place up there. However, the upper reaches of the balcony have a reputation for a smothering atmosphere.

Adding to the mystery is the fact that another theater had stood on the site in the early years of the twentieth century. The Colonial Theater was built in 1909 as a stock company playhouse, soon changing to a moving pictures house. Theater fires were unfortunately common back then, leading the Colonial to tout itself as the "Newest, Handsomest, and Safest" theater in town. True to its word, it did not succumb to fire. Instead, the march of progress was its demise. In 1919, the Colonial Theater was torn down to make way for the AIU Citadel, now known as the Levesque Tower, and the attached Palace Theatre.

The Palace Theatre was the brainchild of vaudeville theater tycoon Edward F. Albee, head of the Keith-Albee vaudeville empire. Albee was a generous man, as committed to helping philanthropic causes as he was to vaudeville. He found ways to incorporate his philanthropic leanings with his love for vaudeville by establishing tuberculosis sanatoriums for vaudeville performers. He also boosted the government's Liberty Bond drive by putting his organization at their disposal. He wanted people to be happy, and he put his big heart into making the Palace a place that would bring smiles to their faces.

The Palace Theatre was indeed a sight to behold. It was designed to resemble the Palais de Versailles in France. Visitors to the new theater were awed by the sweeping marble staircase that met them when they walked into the main lobby. It led up to a floor graced by a glittering fountain and dazzling chandeliers. Architect Thomas Lamb performed a feat that was even more appreciated than the formal beauty of the theater. He laid the theater out so that the acoustics were exceptional. There literally was not a bad seat in the house. For the cinema lovers, motion pictures were mixed in with the vaudeville acts. The needs of the performers were not neglected, either. For their use, there were a laundry, kitchenettes, a nursery and even a fully equipped hospital on site.

In 1929, the Keith-Albee Palace became the RKO (Radio-Keith-Orpheum) Palace. With the advent of talkies, other theaters in town shifted away from stage shows in favor of showing movies. The Palace remained true to Edward Albee's love of vaudeville and became the place in the city to see live stage acts. They had everything from big band orchestras to The Three Stooges. Movies were not completely forgotten, either. In 1942, the Palace was home to the world premiere of *The Male Animal*. That movie, starring Olivia DeHavilland and Henry Fonda, was based on a play by humorist James Thurber. Like Thurston, Thurber was a Columbus native.

The decline of downtown that started in the 1960s brought the Palace Theatre perilously close to an unhappy end. By the early 1980s, the theater was in disrepair and used intermittently at best. Theater historian Phil Sheridan tried to raise awareness of what a treasure the Palace was to its owner, Katherine LeVeque, and to the city of Columbus as a whole. This led to him becoming the general manager of the theater. Staff and volunteers worked long, hard hours to restore the theater to its original beauty. The ultimate goal was also to restore it to financial sustainability. Once renovated, it became home to performances by Opera Columbus, as well as other concerts and productions that came into town. Changes in management policies also increased its financial viability.

In the midst of the restorations, a new threat emerged. There was a push to build a new performing arts center in Columbus. The proponents decided that the older theaters in town would provide too much competition and thus, the Palace Theatre, the historic Southern Theatre and possibly even the Ohio Theatre would have to go. The Columbus Association for the Performing Arts (CAPA) and other groups fought the plan. Thankfully, the Ohio General Assembly let the plan die.

Despite the wonderful changes the Palace had undergone, it was still not earning its keep. After over a decade of considering the matter, Katherine LeVeque effectively transferred ownership of the Palace Theatre to CAPA in 1989. CAPA has managed the theater ever since.

CAPA employees soon discovered that the theater came with some "extras" they hadn't expected. Anna Steffen, who used to work in the theater as one of the maintenance crew, had a perplexing experience there on an otherwise quiet night. She was vacuuming in the balcony of the theater late one night after a performance. The cleaning crew used special vacuums that slung over their shoulders like backpacks to make it easier to maneuver around the stairs and rows of seats. Suddenly, the vacuum she was using shut off. She was annoyed, thinking that she had managed to jerk the cord out from the electric socket. However, when she went up to plug it back in, she found that it was already that way. Then she noticed that the switch on her vacuum

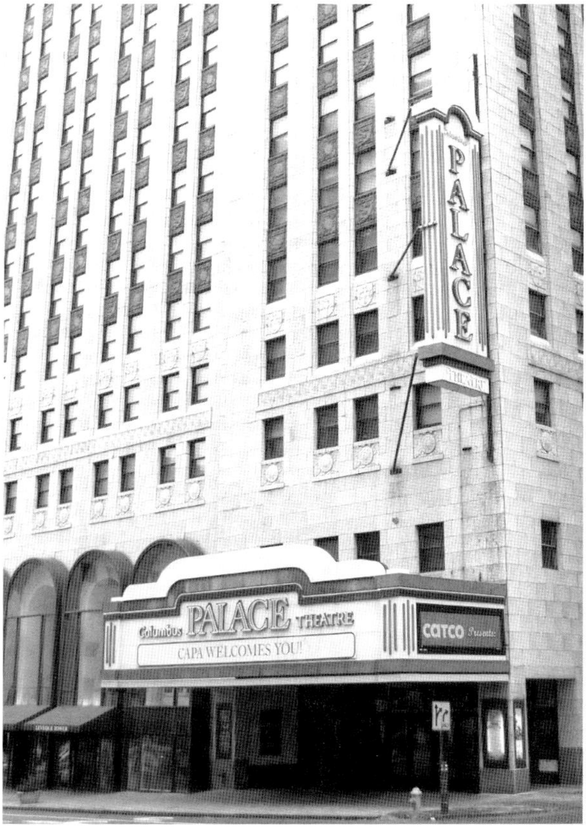

The Palace Theatre was a popular venue for vaudeville acts in the first half of the twentieth century. *Author's collection.*

had been turned off. That was no big deal. She assumed that maybe she had bumped into one of the seats and accidentally turned it off. She went back to vacuuming. A few minutes later, the vacuum stopped working again. She checked the plug once more, a bit less nonchalantly than before, and found that it was still plugged in. She checked the switch. It was turned off. She was sure that she hadn't bumped into anything this time. That made her a little unnerved. She still needed to finish the cleaning, so she switched it back on and went to work. Another fifteen minutes went by before the vacuum turned off again. This time she looked around the theater and decided that it was clean enough.

Chapter 12
Ghosts in Masquerade
Kampmann Costume Company

From the moment you walked into the Kampmann Costume Company, you felt like you were being watched. A row of horror masks stared down with empty eye sockets from where they hung above the shelves. Movie monsters, demons and presidents assessed the newcomers with a hollow gaze. It was unnerving, especially in the fading yellow light of late October evenings. Yet the place also had an air of mystery. Within the glass-fronted shelves lay tiaras and Groucho Marx glasses, clown white and crepe hair, all beckoning the customer to live his fantasy, if only for one night. It was a place of magic.

Situated on South High Street just a couple of blocks south of the statehouse, Kampmann's was a familiar sight to the denizens of downtown Columbus for over a century. While the exact year that Charles Kampmann founded it is unknown, company legend has it that Jenny Lind had visited the shop while she was on her United States tour in 1851. In the early days, it was a grocery on Third Street, a couple of blocks away from its final location on High Street. He expanded it to include imports from Germany to help the local German population feel more at home. The wares included toys, masks and decorations. The masks apparently caught the imagination of his son, also named Charles. Charles Jr., who later changed his name to Carl, was the one who shifted it from being a grocery to being a full-fledged masquerade shop. It wasn't an instant transformation, though. In the intervening years, Carl experimented with running side businesses such as a saloon and a stationery shop. However, it was the costumes that were his true love. By 1887, he was advertising theatrical and masquerade goods, and by 1896, the Kampmann Costume Works was born.

For reasons unclear, Kampmann sold the business to Norwood and Katherine "Queenie" Engle in 1920. However, he could not get his love of costuming out of his system. He started another costume shop, also named Kampmann's. Since the Engles retained the original name of the business that they bought, they were none too happy about this little development. Kampmann was sued over his little faux pas and had to give up the second business. Still pining for his beloved costume shop, Kampmann died in 1924.

He need not have worried about the hands that he left it in. The Kampmann Costume Works flourished under the Engles. They traveled the world to bring home authentic costumes from exotic lands. During the Great Depression, the business actually thrived. People were anxious to forget their worries, and the escape that indulging in masquerades brought them fit the bill. The Engles also started some innovative business ventures. Kampmann's was one of the first companies to manufacture Halloween costumes for children, selling their product as far away as Kansas City. They added gambling devices such as Chuck-a-Lucks and money wheels to rent out for casino parties. It was a prosperous time.

Over the years, Kampmann's had quite a few big-name visitors, from singers and actors to politicians, athletes, clowns and burlesque queens. One of the earliest dignitaries to frequent the shop was humorist James Thurber. Movie actor Bob Cummings stopped by one day, beating the clerk to the punch by saying, "Hey, you look like that Bob Cummings guy!" as soon as he walked in the door. The same clerk recalls that a young Wayne Newton had visited while he was in town to perform. Local TV movie host Flippo the Clown often bought his clown white there. Other celebrity customers included burlesque queen Rose la Rose, mime team Shields and Yarnell, golf professional Jack Nicklaus and longtime Columbus mayor Maynard Edward "Jack" Sensenbrenner.

Russ Duemmel started working at Kampmann's in 1953 as a teenager. Like his predecessors, he soon caught the costuming bug and fell in love with the business. Eventually, when Queenie became old, she sold the place to him.

After the business passed into his hands, Russ started to notice that the business came with a few more perks than he had realized. Based on some of the odd things happening around the shop, it looked suspiciously like there were ghosts. For a business whose busy season was Halloween, that was a happy coincidence.

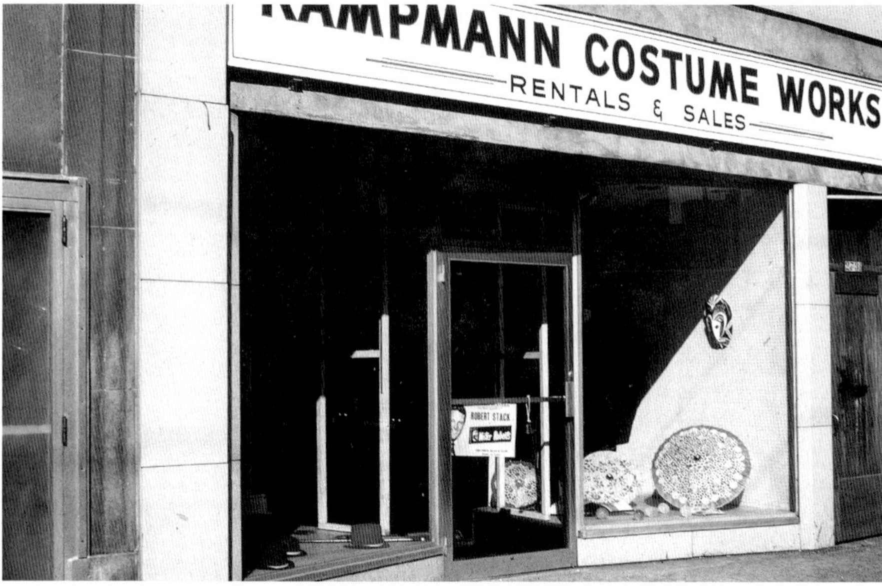

The ever-changing front window of Kampmann Costume Works was a festive sight along South High Street in the 1960s. *Courtesy of Russell Duemmel.*

Most of the ghostly activity around Kampmann's was of the mundane variety. Russ would often arrive in the morning to find lights on that he specifically remembered turning off the night before. He was concerned that he was getting unwelcome visitors of the earthly variety, since Kampmann's was in an unsavory area of downtown. He could never find any other evidence that someone had broken in.

One night, the staff was having their annual end-of-Halloween-season party in the fixed-up end of the basement. The sales area in the basement had the perfect ambiance for a Halloween party. The cases were painted a cheery orange. Even better, the basement was attached to a series of tunnels that ran underneath the streets of Columbus. The front wall of the basement opened into a cavelike area that Russ had transformed into a little mad doctor's office, complete with a Jacob's ladder. As the staff were laughing and enjoying themselves, they heard footsteps coming from the main floor above them. It sounded like a man and a woman, with one set of footsteps being distinctly heavier than the other. They knew it wasn't one of the staff members, since they were all down in that room. Russ got aggravated, thinking that he must not have locked up right and some more customers had slipped in. When he went upstairs, he found that both doors to the outside were indeed locked, and no one was around.

The ghosts also liked to play tricks. Sometimes when Russ was working in the basement, he'd hear someone calling his name from the top of the stairs. He'd assume it was his assistant, Tommy, and would come upstairs to find out what Tommy wanted. He'd find Tommy in a different part of the building, and the guy would claim that he hadn't called him. Then Russ would realize that he hadn't heard any footsteps going away from the stairs. The same thing happened to Tommy a couple of times, too.

One quiet afternoon, Russ was working in the front room when the overhead light started swinging back and forth. It kept swinging very regularly, with metronome-like precision, not slowing down. This had him intrigued because he could see no reason for it to be swinging. He felt the walls to see if there was any vibration. There wasn't any. He went upstairs to see if maybe something going on up there was causing it. He couldn't find anything. When he came back downstairs, the light was still swinging back and forth, as evenly as you please. Finally Russ got on a ladder and caught the light as it swung. He held it still for a minute, then let go. It didn't move again.

Russ's daughter also felt some strange things there. Kampmann's had a lot of clothes in storage that had belonged to the previous owners in decades past. They didn't rent them out because the clothes that survived were often very fragile. Even the sturdier ones were unsuitable for rental. After being refit as hand-me-downs over the years, the old clothes were generally much smaller than the average-size person of today. However, the daughter, who was a teenager at the time, was fairly tiny and was absolutely delighted to find a beautiful old brown dress dating from the 1870s that looked to be her size. She tried it on; it fit perfectly. The moment she stepped into it, though, she got an intense feeling that someone was furious because she was wearing her dress. The daughter had that dress off in record time.

That wasn't the only article of clothing known to have a spirit attached to it. The oldest piece of clothing there, hidden away in a trunk in the basement, was a blue silk gown dating from the 1830s. When a psychic was given a tour of the place, she was immediately drawn to the gown, sensing a spirit hanging around it.

The strangest story about Kampmann's came from a man who was a business associate of the owner. Russ let this man use his office on the weekends to work on a joint venture they were involved in. One Sunday evening, after working there all day, the man gathered up his things to head home. He went out into the hallway that went by the storage area and saw a human-shaped form glowing there. He got the impression that it was a woman. It came toward him and brushed against him as it went by. Instead of feeling the cold of the tomb like he expected, the entity felt hot.

The ghosts got even hotter. In 1989, the shop was destroyed when an arsonist set fire to an adjoining building. It was oddly fitting that the place went up in flames. After all, Kampmann's phone number was 224-HELL.

CHAPTER 13

THE DAPPER SPIRIT

FRANKLIN AVENUE

Chris King has an unusual approach to dealing with ghosts. Instead of screaming or running away, he pours them a drink.

Chris had lived on the historic little street in the Discovery District of Columbus long before he saw the house for sale. The previous owner had died recently. He was an elderly man who had not been able to properly keep the place up for many years; it was an eyesore. The next-door neighbors wanted to buy it to tear it down and put a swimming pool in its place. Chris would have none of that. He loved old buildings and wanted to rescue it. He bought the place himself and spent years turning it into a charming little showplace.

Historic preservationists owe Chris a debt of gratitude for helping preserve the character of the neighborhood. Franklin Avenue represented a different aspect of history than the grander Town Street just to the south. It was lined with modest little Victorian cottages that were home to the servants who worked in the mansions on Town Street. One of the little buildings served as a school for the local children. In the early twentieth century, Grace Kelton joined the two cottages behind her family's mansion for use as a studio for her interior design firm. She also bought seven of the other cottages to rent out to other creative folks in hopes of forming an artists' enclave. The street still has a quiet charm to it, similar to the working-class neighborhoods of German Village.

When one has turned a rundown old house into a beautiful home, the natural inclination is to show it off. Chris had a friend over and was

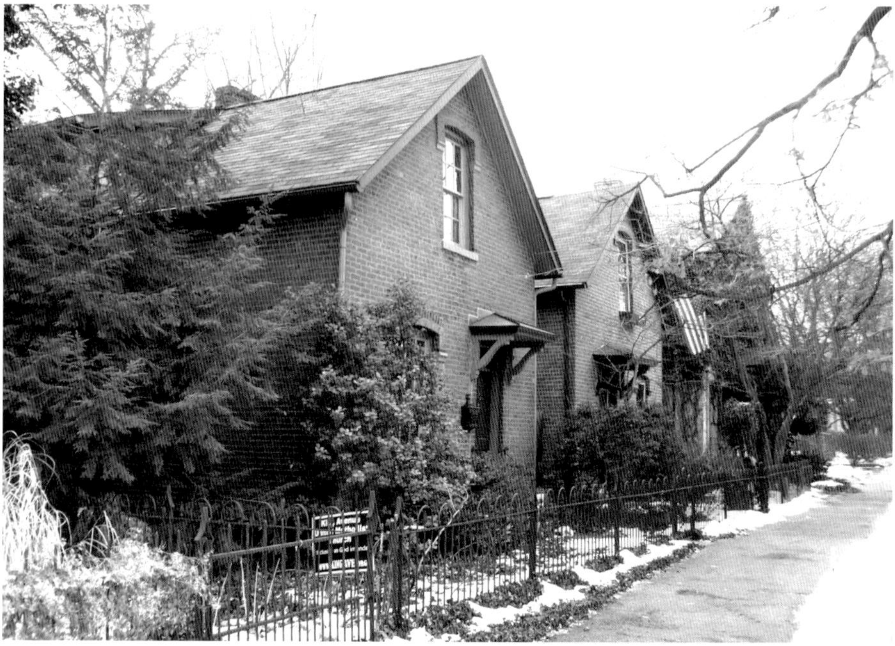

In the twentieth century, there was an attempt by Grace Bird Kelton to turn Franklin Avenue into an artists' colony. *Author's collection.*

showing him all the work he had done on the house. The friend, who was known to be psychically sensitive, was coming down the stairs from the second floor when he stopped and pointed at a chair in the living room. "There's a man there," he announced. Chris was nonchalant. Ever the gracious host, he poured a glass of bourbon and brought it over for his unseen visitor.

Not long afterwards, Chris's partner was quite concerned to come home one day and see a man looking out of the upstairs window. Chris was not supposed to be home yet nor did the man in the window look like him. Ordinarily, he would have assumed it was a burglar, but there was something about the man that had him perplexed. The intruder was wearing a tuxedo. The hair went up on the back of his neck, remembering what the psychic had said. He cautiously entered the house, prepared to take action as needed. However, as he went through the house looking for the interloper, he found that no one else was there.

Seeing the man in the window became a common occurrence. Chris and his partner learned to take the mystery man's presence for granted, but they were curious about who he could be. A ghost in a tuxedo might make sense in the ritzy mansions on Town Street, but why would there be one in a working-class house?

The neighbors were able to clear up the mystery for them. They said that Charles Lockwood, the gentleman who had owned the house before they did, was a bartender for the Shriners. His job required him to wear a tuxedo to work. He also got a lift to work every day with a coworker. When he was alive, it was not uncommon to see him looking out the window, waiting for his ride.

Chris has moved on to live in yet another house on Franklin Avenue. Since he lives just down the street, he passes by his old house on a daily basis. From what he's seen, his old ghostly roommate is still there, still waiting for his long overdue ride.

CHAPTER 14

THE RIVER OF DEATH

FRANKLINTON

The Scioto River played an integral part in the history of Franklinton, the first settlement in the area. It surrounds Franklinton on three sides and is, in fact, the reason for Franklinton's existence. Over the centuries, the Scioto has deposited rich fertile soil along its western bank, building up the bend in the river where Franklinton sits. When Lucas Sullivant, the city founder, saw how rich the soil was here, he knew this was the place he wanted to settle.

The Scioto has its mysteries. In the river near where the Old Franklinton Cemetery is today, there used to be an island known as British Island or, more ominously, as Bloody Island. It was washed away long ago, but in Franklinton's early years, it was large enough to be put to use. During the War of 1812, British prisoners were housed there. Ohio's fierce summers and harsh winters were particularly hard on the prisoners, as they were used to the milder English climate. They also suffered from diseases that were raging through the area at the time. Many decided that their chances of survival were better if they tried to escape. That didn't work out as planned. Sharpshooters were stationed near the island and would shoot the escapees as they tried to swim to freedom. To this day, people report hearing ghostly splashes and screams as the British soldiers attempt to break free of their eternal prison.

The island may have had a darker history even before that. Rumor has it that it was the site of a massacre committed by one Native American tribe on another. Old stories tell of the cries of women and children being heard there in the empty woods.

Then there was the Flood of 1913. Being on a flood plain, floods were nothing new in Franklinton. They had at least ten minor floods in their history previous to this one. One in 1794 was more fierce, and it nearly wiped out the fledgling settlement. Hardy souls that they were, the residents of Franklinton cleared away the damage, rebuilt their town and went on with their lives. They felt that they could survive anything. However, the flood in 1913 took them completely by surprise.

It was a dreary Easter Sunday. The previous few days had been nice and balmy, lulling everyone into thinking they'd have a pleasant spring. Then the rain started to fall, and the rain kept coming. There was a brief respite overnight, causing the *Columbus Dispatch* to cheerfully report on Monday that Columbus need not fear the storms that had been ravaging the Midwest. Obviously, the worst of the weather was passing by. But they were wrong. Three inches had fallen, and the rain still came. Five inches had fallen, and the rain still came. Seven inches fell, and the rain kept coming. In the end, nine inches had fallen. Nine inches of rain in a short time is never a good thing. It's even worse when you live on a flood plain.

On Tuesday morning, the levees broke. The residents were greeted with a wondrous sight: a wall of water, like Moses parting the Red Sea. The trouble was, the wall was heading toward them. It hit with such a force that it toppled over entire buildings and swept away residents standing in the street, dumbfounded by their imminent doom.

Things became even more dire when the supports of the bridges groaned and creaked under the strain. The residents knew that their only escape route was about to be cut off. One by one, throughout the morning, the bridges crumbled and fell into the wash. One streetcar full of desperate people came to the Town Street Bridge as it was undergoing its death throes. A police man tried to turn it back, explaining that the bridge was about to collapse. The passengers begged and pleaded to cross, fearing that they would be killed if they didn't. The policeman relented and allowed them to pass. He yelled at the conductor to "gun it," and the streetcar sped across the bridge like lightning. Just as they reached the safety of the far bank, the bridge tore apart and fell into the grim waters. Other streetcars were not so lucky. An entire streetcar full of passengers got caught in the floodwater and was pulled down, drowning all aboard.

They weren't safe in their homes, either. Some residents thought that they could ride out the flood in their houses, like they had in the past, staying in the upper floors until the waters receded. What they hadn't counted on was the force of the current. Imagine the horror of having refused rescue,

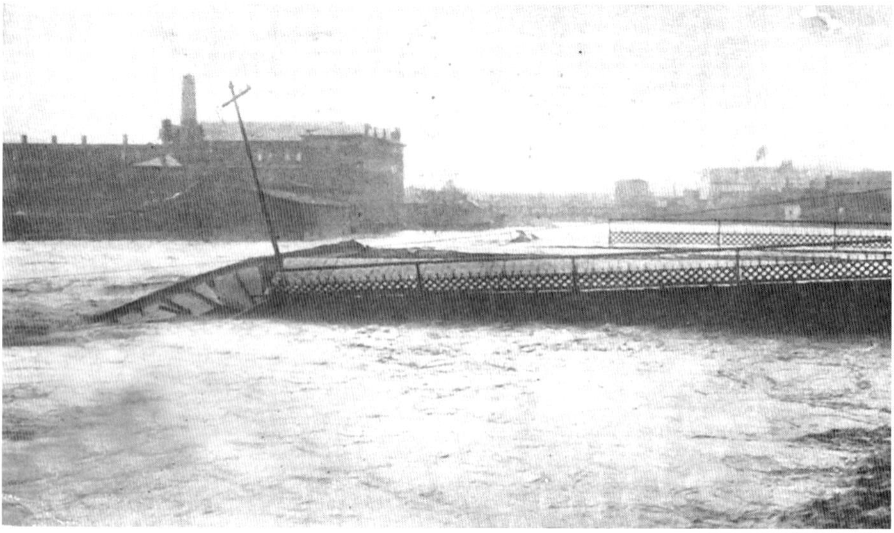

One streetcar full of passengers made a narrow escape during the collapse of the Town Street Bridge during the Flood of 1913. *Author's collection.*

thinking you were safe in your house, only for it to slowly crumble around you and drag you into the depths.

Some residents knew that their houses were in danger of being knocked over by the force of the water, so they climbed into trees for safety. Throughout the day, their neighbors heard their pitiful calls for help. As the evening came, the calls grew fewer and fewer as the victims became cold and weak. The night was met with the eerie sound of water swirling about, punctuated by the screams and splashes of the weary falling from their perches into the depths below.

The rain finally stopped on Wednesday, but that gave the residents of Franklinton no relief. In its place came sleet and snow, adding another torment to the half-drowned citizens.

When the Columbus Landmarks Foundation was putting together a ghost tour of Franklinton, a medium was brought through to see what he could find out from the flood victims. He spoke with some individuals, and in one case, an entire family of ghosts who had been killed in the flood. Almost one hundred years after the fact, they were inevitably still shell shocked by the horror of their experience and agitated over having their lives cut short. The ghosts are haunted by the memories of being pulled under the murky water and swept away.

Other tales told by the survivors were equally bone chilling. One eyewitness who had been a little girl at the time told this sad story: as her own family was awaiting rescue from their house, she saw her neighbor, Mrs. Copeland, climb into a trunk and set off in the torrents. Mrs. Copeland thought it would work as a makeshift boat to help her get to her daughter. Her little boat tossed and swirled in the eddies and then was swept away by the current. Mrs. Copeland was never seen again, alive or dead.

It seems that Mrs. Copeland is still around, though. When the medium was given her name, he immediately picked up on the fact that she was missing, it was a tragedy, her body was never found and that she was upset about it. After talking to her for a few minutes, he was able to get the full story out of her. She had found her daughter, but the current was pulling the trunk away too fast for her to get to the woman. She thought that she would have a better chance swimming, so she jumped into the icy flow. Unfortunately, the current was still too strong for her. She drowned. As her body got dragged along, her foot became caught in the wreckage of the State Street Bridge, close to where the amphitheater by the Center of Science and Industry is now. She has been there ever since.

Having claimed its victims, the floodwater transformed into the river of the dead. A flotilla of corpses was carried gently down by the water to Green Lawn Cemetery, as if it knew that would be their final resting place. Other bodies were found as far away as Portsmouth, the deceased having made one last macabre journey far from home.

Even once the waters receded, the horror didn't end. Franklinton was littered with the grim aftermath of the flood. The streets were impassable from all the sidewalk and fence planks that had been dislodged. Entire streetcars and houses were turned over. The worst part was the dismembered bodies that remained scattered among the debris, all covered in a thick brown slime. Souvenir postcards were produced, some with gruesome notes written on them to detail how many bodies had been found in the shot. In Green Lawn Cemetery, dead bodies were found scattered among the old graves. The *Columbus Dispatch* reported that at least two truckloads of bodies had been gathered up and taken to makeshift morgues. It was a city of death.

The people of Franklinton have a strong spirit. Over the years, they rebuilt their town, living and thriving in it. Yet one has to wonder if they aren't just a little nervous any time it rains. Maybe on some dark stormy night, they have heard the splashes and screams of the doomed falling from the trees or looked out their windows to see the ghost of Mrs. Copeland floating past in her little makeshift boat.

CHAPTER 15

QUIET SOULS

THE OHIO STATE UNIVERSITY MAIN LIBRARY

When most people think of ghosts in libraries, the scene from *Ghostbusters* immediately comes to mind. After all, doesn't every librarian secretly dream of spending her afterlife shushing people? According to the staff at The Ohio State University's main library, it isn't the spirits of librarians that are the problem. It is the other ghosts hanging around. They should know. They have had plenty of experience with them.

Just looking at the Thompson Library, one would not guess that it is rife with ghostly activity. Behind the glittering glass façade, there is so much action already from the living. Students and professors swarm through the building, industriously searching the stacks for just the right piece of information or hanging out in the coffee bar that was put in to give them a more relaxed place to study. The staff is kept busy aiding them in their research or reshelving the mountains of books that are returned every day. For a place that is thought of as being quiet, it is always abuzz with energy.

The Ohio State University's main library was always a busy place. The first library was originally housed in the Main Building, later known as University Hall. The room was lined with walnut cases for the books and had a small table at which the librarian worked. Additional reading tables were located in the Geological Room. By 1882, the student newspaper was lamenting about how noisy and overcrowded it had become. Two years later, the library was moved upstairs to the third floor, replacing the Botanical Department, which now had its own building. It held 2,402 volumes and 28 periodicals. Within a year, they were already outgrowing the space, especially in terms of the reading room.

The library had constraints in other respects. Blue-gray book plates indicated that the books could only be checked out during a half-hour period two days a week with a two-week checkout period. A limit of two books could be checked out at a time, and reference materials were noncirculating. When the library moved to the third floor, even books taken from the shelves to read in the library had to be signed out due to theft. The "closed reserve" system was also instituted.

In addition to theft, it seems that the students were not as well behaved as one might expect from proper Victorians. The library was used as a social center, with groups such as the female students' Browning Society meeting there and other individuals hanging out to chat. Noise levels were an issue. There were complaints of graffiti done in pencil on the walls, tables and chairs, as well as markings inside the books. Likewise, there were problems with students moving books in order to prop their feet up on the shelves. A more curious concern was that students were leaving their shoes on the window sills, "as if to advertise them for sale." The aggravations did not stop at the university's library. After students complained about how limited and overly advanced the book selection was at the university's library, they were given permission to use the state library. This proved to be a headache for the librarian there. The students' presence led to an upsurge in damage to the books, as they had a nasty habit of cutting out the pages for their own use.

Professor Joseph Millikin was the first college librarian, with another professor as his assistant librarian. Their library work was only a part-time responsibility, secondary to their teaching. During the tenure of the second college librarian, Josiah Renick Smith, they started using students as the assistant librarian. Mary Frank Morrison, who also became the first woman to graduate from Ohio State, was made the first student assistant librarian in 1878. Female students in this position became the norm for the next ten years. When they started employing additional student workers in 1891, they added male students to the staff.

In 1887, Olive Branch Jones became the assistant librarian, starting a long and fruitful association with the library that lasted until her death. She was lauded for learning the special skills involved in running a library despite not having professional training in it. In 1893, she was promoted to being librarian, under a move to have a professional librarian in that role instead of just a faculty member. Even with her not having completed her undergraduate degree, the trustees had faith that she was the right person for the job. The following decades proved that she was.

Jones had big challenges ahead of her. The same year that she became librarian, the library was moved to larger, "temporary" housing in Orton Hall. The tenure there ended up being less temporary than expected. The library stayed in Orton Hall until a new building was built specifically to house the collections nineteen years later. Under her leadership, the library open hours were increased to over eighty hours, the staff to more than twenty-five employees and the holdings to over 300,000 volumes.

The new building was luxurious compared to what the students had been used to. One student described it as being "too wonderful and pleasurable to be honestly realized." The library was arranged around a large reference hall where students had full access to the books, surrounded by closed stacks into which only library staff, advanced students and researchers were allowed. It had a few different specialized library rooms, as well as lecture rooms, seminar rooms and a study area. Miss Jones, however, was disappointed that the trustees had decided to cut costs and built the library for less than half of what they had originally planned. In the process, her suggestions on how to make it more easily expandable in the future had been ignored. Her concerns were not unfounded. By 1920—a mere seven years after the library had been built—it was already filled to capacity.

Earl N. Manchester took over as librarian in 1928 and eventually became the director of libraries. He was admired for his kind smile, gentlemanly ways and intimate knowledge of the libraries' collections. His good humor came in handy while dealing with the capacity issues. The library reached critical mass just as the Great Depression hit, making funding for expansion a distant dream. As a dubious benefit, the funding cuts also slowed down the rate at which new books were being acquired. The overcrowding issue in the main library was resolved by shifting books to the nine departmental libraries. Unfortunately, that caused the departmental libraries to now be overcrowded. Finally in 1949, work began on an addition to the main library. The library was renamed the William Oxley Thompson Memorial Library, now shortened to Thompson Library. When it was completed in 1952, the undoubtedly exhausted Mr. Manchester retired.

As with many aspects of the university, some things never change. Eventually, the books and periodicals housed in the library outgrew the capacity. The library built an addition to the back in 1977. That helped for awhile, but the storage issue soon reared its ugly head again. Instead of expanding the main library, the university library system took a different

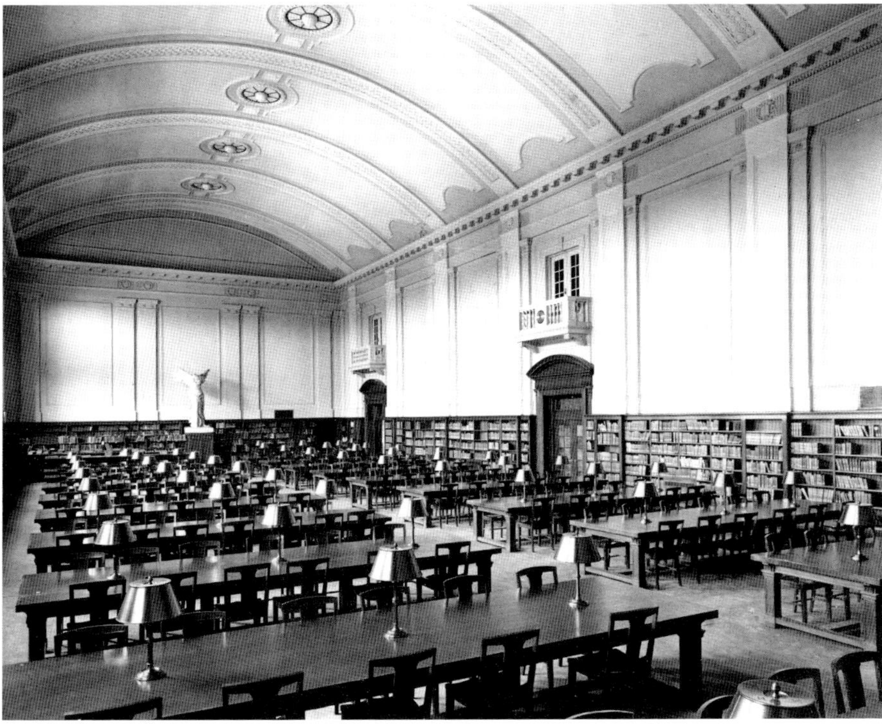

After years of having the library in cramped quarters, the reading room in The Ohio State University's main library was designed to be spacious. *The Ohio State University Archives.*

approach in the 1990s. An offsite storage facility was built to keep books that were in less demand. If a student or faculty member wanted them, they could always be retrieved as needed, usually within half a day of the request. The new book depository used a high-density storage system that allowed them to keep as many books as possible in the smallest amount of space. Even at that rate, they had to expand the facility only six years after it was built.

It didn't take long for Richard Thames (name changed upon request) to realize that something was odd about the library when he first started working there as a student in the 1990s. He was assigned to a team that worked on the seventh floor, putting away books and making sure the stacks were in order. He frequently felt like someone was watching him, and it wasn't just his coworkers checking up on the new guy. Richard also noticed that he often felt like someone was walking around him when he was the only one in the area.

Initially, Richard's coworkers were reluctant to talk about the strange activity in the stacks. One by one, they would shyly bring up the topic when no one else was around. It became sort of an open secret. As time went on, the student workers developed a little initiation ritual for new staff members. They would send the new workers into one of the most haunted areas by themselves without having warned them first. Then they would patiently wait for the new worker to come back with a perturbed look on her or his face.

Richard's coworkers mentioned that they sometimes heard footsteps walk around the floor when they were the only ones there. Due to the way sound traveled on the floor, it was pretty easy to tell when a living being was there. There would be the telltale sounds of the elevator stopping at the floor or the doors from the stairwell area opening. The mysterious footsteps were heard without the usual accompanying noises. It was odder still that the footsteps would sound like they were close by, right behind the staff member. When they weren't hearing footsteps, the sound of whispers and voices also kept them in uneasy company.

They might have been able to brush that off as their imagination, if it hadn't been for the fact that the book carts moved by themselves. A skeptic might theorize that the carts moved because gravity caused them to roll slightly on the old floors that were probably uneven from years of use. However, the book carts were so heavy that it took a bit of effort to make them move. It would be hard to explain why the carts moved several feet at a time. Another perplexing abnormality was that the books occasionally fell off the shelves by themselves. The books were tucked securely onto the shelves, held in place by the other books surrounding them. There was no logical explanation for them to just pop off of the shelves.

This had most of the workers a bit freaked out. Richard took a more laissez faire approach to it. He emphasizes, "I never felt anything menacing. If anything, it felt like it was just trying to get our attention." Richard tried to communicate with the spirit telepathically and let it know that he wasn't trying to hurt it. He told it mentally that he just wanted to coexist peacefully. Richard admits, "I felt sort of a sense of relief after that."

After awhile, Richard noticed that a lot of the activity occurred near a padlocked cage in the northeast corner of the floor. No one was really sure what it was there for, as it only seemed to contain more books. Richard noticed shadows moving around the "book jail" from the corner of his eyes. It was tempting to pass that off as just an optical illusion. Then one day, he saw something that threw him for a loop. There, standing by the cage, was the shadow of a man in hat, holding a book as if he were reading it. Richard was about thirty feet away, so he started walking toward the shadow to get a closer look. As he approached, the shadow seemed to disappear into the cage.

Richard was intrigued by his ghostly companion and grew to be comfortable around him. Later on, when he was working alone on that floor, he felt a tapping on his shoulder as if someone were trying to get his attention. Instead of being spooked, he calmly told the spirit, "Oh yeah, I'm aware of you."

Other staff members were not so easygoing when the spirit tried to get their attention. They were unnerved when the heavy padlock on the cage would swing noiselessly without anyone near to have bumped into it. A security guard had second thoughts about his job when he saw the padlock lift up on its own and slam back down.

Eventually, some student workers became so curious about the cage that they tried to break into it. They didn't succeed, but that seemed to heighten the activity. Richard finally asked his supervisors what was the deal with the cage. He was told that it contained books that had been donated by a professor who passed away. That was just a temporary holding area for them. Of course, the cage wasn't the normal holding area for books. Eventually the books were moved, and the cage itself was dismantled. After that, the activity slowed down. It eventually stopped altogether. The last few times Richard was there, he didn't sense anything around there anymore. He couldn't tell whether it had moved on to another plane of existence or just moved to a different part of the library.

Richard started working on other floors only to find that they held their own spooks. The fourth floor was especially creepy. It was extra dark up there due to the lack of windows. The books stored on that floor also were not on subjects that pertained to many students. The floor was generally deserted aside from the students who went up there to engage in promiscuous activity. The worst part was the unwelcoming vibe that Richard felt when he was up there. He was working there shelving books by himself one day when he saw someone out of the corner of his eye passing by in the aisle. As with the seventh floor, it was impossible for anyone to get onto the floor without making noise to announce their arrival. He walked out to the aisle to see if maybe there really was someone there. There was no one around, so he went back to work. A few minutes later, he saw someone pass by again, coming from the same direction as before. Richard was overcome with a feeling of dread. He sat back down on the floor to work. This time he purposely kept an eye on the aisle, while trying to make it look like his attention was on the books. The ruse worked. Soon, an apparition appeared in the aisle. It was shaped like a man, but there was something grotesquely wrong about him. Not only were his arms unnaturally long and thin, they undulated in a flowing, rhythmic wave.

Richard's boss had a hard time understanding his reluctance to continue working on that floor, but the second in command was more sympathetic. She had likewise had strange experiences on the various floors. Hers were more of a friendly nature. When she was on the third floor, she would see little balls of light dancing around. It wasn't unusual for them to lead her to a point in the stacks where she would find a long-missing book that had been misplaced. She didn't know who the ghost was, but there is a good bet that it was a fellow librarian.

One of the spirits there was more concrete, at least in appearance. One quarter during finals week, Richard and a female coworker were working on the third floor on the north wing. His coworker had gone downstairs, so he was surprised when he looked up to see what he thought was her standing by his book cart. The young woman had shoulder-length hair like his coworker but had her back turned so he couldn't see her face. Richard realized that she was someone else. She walked toward the windows, which was a dead end. He had an odd feeling about her, so he followed. She was not there. She did not seem to have gone around the corner, which led to another room, but he checked in there, anyway. The young woman was not to be found. After thinking about it, he knew why she had intrigued him so. While she looked as solid as any normal human being, she was washed out, as if he had been looking at her through a fog.

Another day, he was working with a male coworker in an adjoining room. They were done with their shift and were just shooting the breeze. His friend got distracted at one point and kept looking beyond Richard at an area that led to the other room. Richard asked him what he was looking at. Not surprisingly, he said a girl. The coworker saw her go around the corner, so he followed her. He soon came back, saying that the girl had mysteriously disappeared. When Richard asked him what she looked like, he described a girl with shoulder-length hair who seemed somewhat faded.

Things have changed a bit since Richard worked there. The library has since undergone extensive renovations. At nearly one hundred years old, the library building was beginning to show its age. It no longer fit the needs of the current users and modern technologies as well as one would hope. After

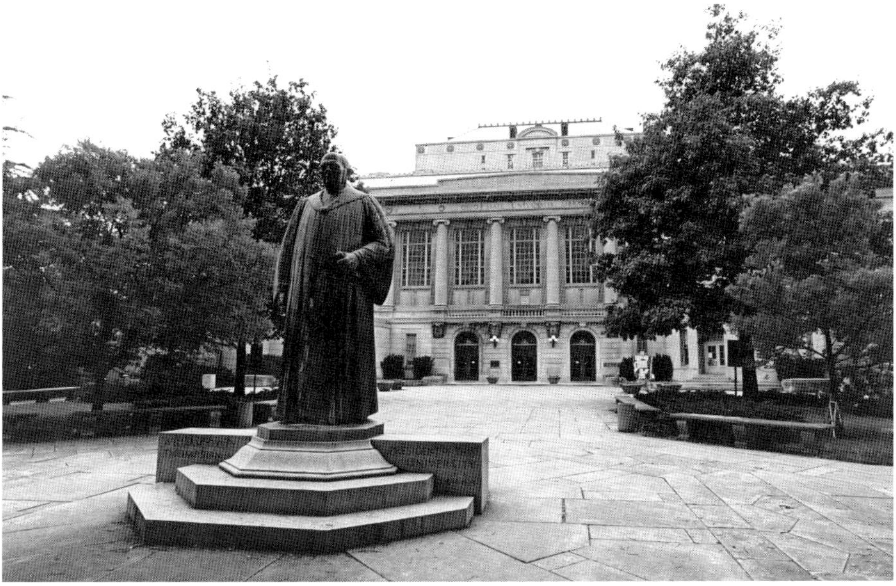

The Ohio State University's main library was renamed the Willam Oxley Thompson Memorial Library after one of the early university presidents. *The Ohio State University Archives.*

a massive facelift, the improved library opened in 2009. Some of the earlier additions had been demolished and replaced. Two stunning changes were an extension that was added to one side of the building and a central atrium brightened by a huge section of skylights. Created largely from glass, both were designed to be environmentally responsible, making use of natural light as much as possible. However, care was given to preserve the original 1913 building. The old grand reading room was restored to look very much as it had been when the library first opened.

Olive Branch Jones might not even recognize her beloved library behind the glass and open spaces. Yet one has to wonder if she isn't still hanging around in spirit, keeping an eye on the place and helping her successors find wayward books.

CHAPTER 16

WHEN THE LIGHTS GO OUT

OHIO THEATRE

Across the street from the statehouse lies the most exuberant of the theaters in Columbus. Dressed in gold and rich reds, the Ohio Theatre has a personality like Auntie Mame: bold, confident and ready to have a good time.

Thomas Lamb, the architect who designed her, wanted to make it an experience to see the theater, not just to see what was playing on the screen. He reasoned that "the theater is the palace of the average man. As long as he is there, it is his, and it helps him lift himself out of his daily drudgery." Happily, theater magnate Morris Loew agreed, sparing no expense in creating the splendor that makes the Ohio Theater so bewitching. Gold stars strewn across the red sky of the ceiling evoke the magic of the Arabian nights. Sumptuous Spanish-Moorish arches and twisted columns further draw the viewer into a mystical world. Even the downstairs lounge was exotic, with zebra skins pinned to the walls. Fittingly, when the divine Ohio Theatre opened for business on March 17, 1928, the main feature was the Greta Garbo movie *The Divine Woman*.

Movies were not the only thing on the program that day. The Ohio Theatre also featured the stage show *Milady's Fans*. Stage shows were a staple at the Ohio Theatre in the early years in addition to the movies. In order to accommodate the needs for the silent movies and the stage shows, the Ohio Theatre had its own nineteen-member orchestra. The old conductor stand, complete with a gauge to let him know how far along they were in the movie, can still be seen in the upstairs ladies' lounge. Eventually, talkies replaced

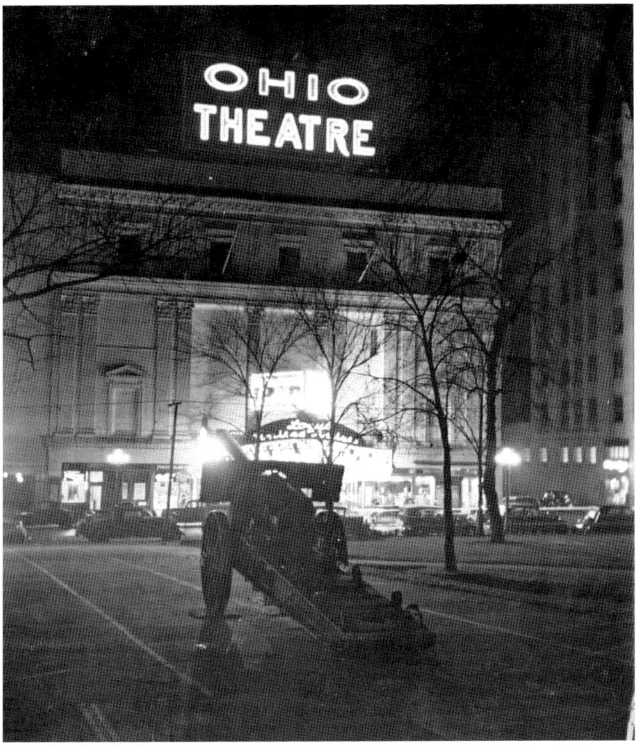

The Ohio Theatre is the most elaborate and probably most haunted of the downtown theaters. *Courtesy of the Ohio Historical Society.*

the silents, and the Ohio Theatre phased out stage shows in favor of movies. After that, the orchestra pit fell silent for decades.

Like its downtown neighbor, the Palace Theatre, the Ohio Theatre was a celebrity on its own for a night. In 1945, it was the site of the world premiere of *Captain Eddie*, a 20th Century-Fox film about the life of World War I flying ace and Columbus native Edward "Eddie" Vernon Rickenbacker. Captain Eddie Rickenbacker and his wife were the guests of honor, attended by Governor Frank J. Lausche, Mayor James A. Rhodes and the former governor, John W. Bricker. While the film's star, Fred MacMurray, was not able to make it, Columbusites still flocked to the theater to catch a glimpse of other Hollywood celebrities such as Lloyd Nolan and Carole Landis.

Once its glamour days were over, the Ohio Theatre nearly became a ghost. As suburbia became the place to live in Columbus in the 1950s and '60s, downtown Columbus fell into decline. Fewer people lived downtown or thought it was worth the drive to take advantage of the amenities there. Business for the old downtown theaters fell off, and by the late 1960s, the Ohio Theatre stood empty.

The Columbus Association for the Performing Arts, more commonly known as CAPA, started a campaign in 1969 to keep the Ohio Theatre from being demolished. The situation was dire to the point where two previous attempts to save the building had failed. CAPA's efforts evolved into a project to completely restore the Ohio and turn it into a working theater once more. They bought both the Ohio Theatre and the Grand Theatre, which shared a wall with the Ohio. Unfortunately, the Grand had to be razed. CAPA took advantage of the empty space on the east side of the building where the Grand used to be by adding the Galbreath Pavilion. That now houses extra lobby and rehearsal space and office areas on the upper floors. The stage house and orchestra pit were enlarged, and additional dressing room and loading dock space were added to the back. The end result is a theater that is just as grand and even more spacious than it had been in its early years. Thanks to CAPA, the Ohio Theatre is once more one of Columbus's greatest treasures. It is now filled with delighted audiences that have come to see the Columbus Symphony Orchestra, Broadway shows and a summer classic movie series that hearkens back to its earlier days.

Like any good theater, the Ohio Theatre has its share of ghosts. The place is rumored to be haunted by the spirit of an old lady who frequents the balcony. She has been seen by some of the cleaning staff over the years. It is thought that this spirit dates back to the days when the Ohio Theatre ran motion pictures all day long. It was common for people to come there to make a day of it, watching movies from morning until dinner time. On the other hand, the upper balcony seats have the best acoustics, which suggests that she may be more of a symphony fan.

Another haunting is said to be a small child who has been heard laughing in the basement. One of the Columbus Symphony Orchestra musicians once brought his psychic niece on a tour of the building. She felt something really disturbing in the orchestra pit in the basement and refused to enter it.

The child may have come from an earlier time period than the theater. Before the Ohio Theatre was even a twinkle in Thomas Lamb's eye, the site already had a rich history. The Columbus City Hall had been built there shortly after the Civil War ended. It was home to a historic meeting in 1890 between delegates from the National Progressive Union and the Knights of Labor District Trades Assembly 135 that resulted in the formation of United Mine Workers of America. Generations of Columbus's movers and shakers passed legislation there that shaped the city's future. Rich history or not, the building did not keep up with Columbus's desire for modernity. By the dawn of the Jazz Age, the building's heavy-handed Gothic design had lost its

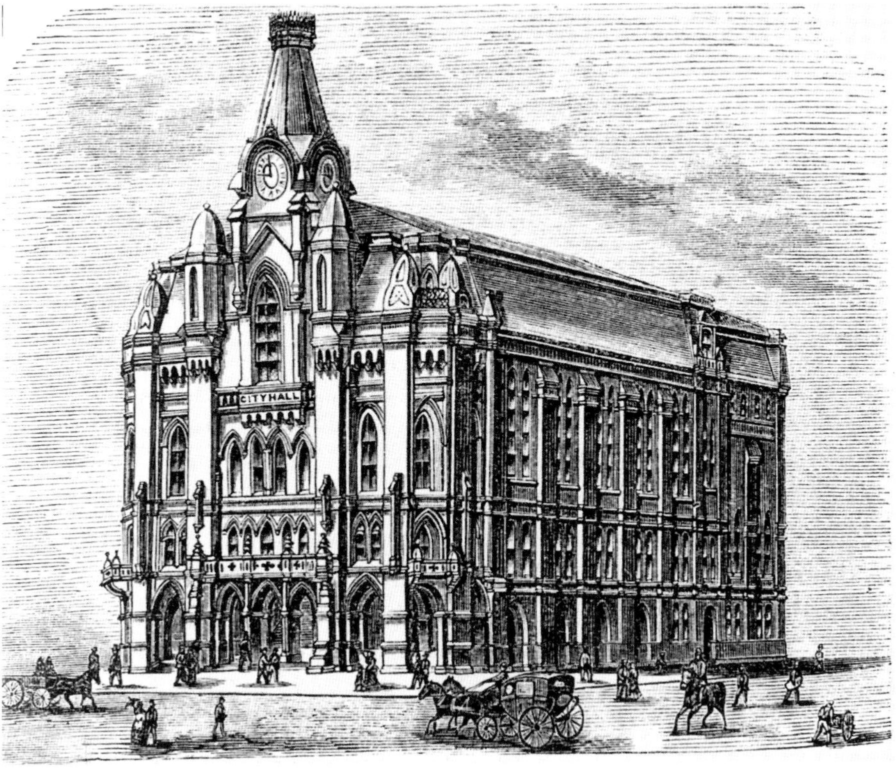

The old Columbus City Hall was originally on the site where the Ohio Theatre now stands. *Courtesy of the Columbus Metropolitan Library.*

aesthetic appeal. As tends to happen to public buildings in Columbus when there is political motivation to replace it with a new one, the Columbus City Hall mysteriously went up in flames in 1921.

The most prominent ghost at the Ohio Theatre is Charlie, an old stage manager who worked there in the mid-twentieth century. Mention his name around the longtime stagehands, and you are bound to be met with a round of grumbles. He had a reputation for being a bit of a perfectionist, which did not always sit well with his coworkers. It doesn't help that Charlie is still very much at work. When he finds that a stagehand hasn't done things to his satisfaction, he makes sure to let them know. It isn't unusual that when a stagehand has left a prop out a little too long, he will go through a frantic round of searching for it only to find it moved to a nonsensical place.

Many times when the symphony's ticket office staff was working late on the fifth floor of the Galbreath Pavilion, they would hear the right-side elevator come up. When the doors opened, no one would be there. They couldn't figure out how one of the elevators could come up in the first place, as the security staff locks them after closing the building to the public for the night. Once locked, people can come down on them, but no one can come up. The old stagehands claimed that that was Charlie's doing. One of the symphony employees got into the habit of saying hello to Charlie whenever she came in the building. After awhile, the elevator on the right would frequently open by itself whenever she came into the lobby. No one can say that Charlie isn't quite the gentleman. He may not be able to hold doors for ladies, but he will hold elevators.

Charlie has actually been seen by Anna Steffen, one of the security guards. She was closing up at the end of her shift late one night and saw the reflection of a man in the glass doors to the left of the security desk. The man would have had to have been standing in the door to the hallway that leads to backstage. She did a thorough search of the place and couldn't find anyone in the building. When she described the man the next day to the longtime stagehands, sure enough, he fit the description of Charlie.

The ticket office staff had a couple of staff members who were firm believers in ghosts. Often when they saw the elevator doors open by themselves that would start a discussion about it. Another staff member, Wayne, was a staunch skeptic. One time, when he was spouting off about how much he didn't believe in ghosts, the light above him blew out. Wayne sputtered that that was just a coincidence and that he still didn't believe in ghosts. He quit not too long after that for a better career opportunity. From then on, in the course of such discussions, a light would explode any time someone mentioned Wayne. The maintenance men hated him for blowing their light bulb budget. Even a few years after Wayne left, saying his name still produced a light bulb explosion.

The experiences they had intrigued one of them enough to bring in a Ouija board. They weren't expecting much but decided to give it a try. Two of the staff members were touching the planchette, while a third staff member, Jack, asked it questions. Rhonda Maynard, a former ticket office manager for the symphony, admits that the results surprised them when Jack told them to ask the board where he was born. She said, "It started spelling C-A-. I interrupted and said, 'Ha! Jack was born in West Virginia. See, it's fake!' Jack had a funny look on his face. He said, 'I was born in a car.' No one knew that. He swore it was true. I don't know if he was pulling our leg or not, but all of us became believers."

Rhonda particularly felt weird vibes in the second-floor ladies lounge. It felt OK on performance nights when there were a lot of people around, but when the theater was empty, the lounge still felt occupied. One time when she was giving a tour of the theater to a new employee, one of them noticed the coat check room across the hall from the lounge. The new employee asked what it was. They tried the door to the room and surprisingly found it unlocked. Much to Rhonda's discomfort, the unsettling vibes were even stronger in there. They giggled at how silly they felt and asked, "Is there anyone in there?" There wasn't any answer. They still felt creeped out enough that they decided they'd spent enough time there. When they switched off the light, a bunch of hangers fell to the floor, accompanied by a crashing noise. They nervously laughed at the "coincidence" but shut the door and got away from there as quickly as possible.

Another night, after the rest of the office staff had left, Rhonda and another one of the believers from the ticket office decided to take the office Ouija board into the ladies' lounge for fun. The atmosphere in the lounge was very unnerving, but they weren't getting any answers to their questions. Eventually, they moved the planchette to "Goodbye" to end their session. The planchette swung firmly over to "NO." They tried saying goodbye again. It jerked back to "NO." They tried several more times to end the session, but the planchette kept insistently sliding back to "NO." The feeling in the room became intensely disturbing, and once again, they fled.

Brave souls that they were, they decided to take the Ouija board into the theater late one night a few weeks later. It was pitch dark in the theater in general, so they stayed in one of the stairwells by a doorway that looked into the lower balcony of the theater. They started off with the usual "Is anyone there?" kind of questions. After a few minutes, the planchette began moving. They asked questions relating to their workplace: "Do you like the Columbus Symphony Orchestra?" "Do you like classical music?" "Who is your favorite composer?" Wagner is apparently the ghostly composer of choice. The staff had heard about an audience member who died of a heart attack in the theater during a performance in the 1980s, so they asked if their newfound friend was dead. It said "yes." Then they asked how it died, and the planchette started circling wildly. They were getting a little freaked out, but they continued with another question: "Did you die of a heart attack?" The planchette came to a dead stop. They were quite frightened by this point, yet still not ready to leave. They felt a strong presence near and scanned the darkness for any sign of life. No living soul was around but them.

Then they asked the scariest question of all:

"Do you know Wayne?"

Bibliography and References

Books

Andromeda, Sandy, and Leslie Blankenship. *Death and Destruction Strike Columbus, Ohio.* Columbus, OH: North Liberty Publications, 1996.

Birnes, William J., and Joel Martin. *The Haunting of America.* New York: Tom Doherty Associates, LLC, 2009.

Chase, Salmon Portland, and John Niven. *The Salmon P. Chase Papers.* Kent, OH: Kent State University Press, 1993.

A Citizen of Ohio. *Interior Causes of the War: The Nation Demonized, and Its President a Spirit-Rapper.* New York: M. Doolady, 1863.

Clark, Uriah. *Plain Guide to Spiritualism.* Boston, MA: William White and Company, 1863.

Cole, Charles C., Jr. *A Fragile Capital: Identity and the Early Years of Columbus, Ohio.* Columbus: Ohio State University Press, 2001.

Crowe, Catherine. *The Night-side of Nature; or, Ghosts and Ghost-seers.* New York: J.S. Redfield, Clinton Hall, 1850.

Directory of the City of Columbus, for the Year 1848, Containing a Brief History of the City, Statistics of Institutions, and the Names, Residence and Business of All Citizens, Inhabitants, &c. Columbus, OH: John Siebert, 1848.

Drake, Benjamin. *Life of Tecumseh and of His Brother the Prophet; with a Historical Sketch of the Shawanoe Indians.* Cincinnati, OH: H.M. Rulison, Queen City Publishing House, 1856.

Edwards, Linden F. *Body Snatching in Ohio during the Nineteenth Century.* Fort Wayne, IN: Public Library of Fort Wayne and Allen County, 1955.

Forman, Jonathan. *The First Cholera Epidemic in Columbus, Ohio (1833).* New York: P.B. Hoeber, 1934.

Franklin County Historical and Genealogical Society. *Franklin County, Ohio 1872 Historical Atlas and Plat Maps 1842, 1846, 1883 Indexed.* Columbus, OH: Franklin County Historical and Genealogical Society, 1998.

Franklin County Infirmary. *Patient Register, 1867–1953.* Ohio Historical Society, Columbus.

Gehlbach, D.R. *The Archaeology of Franklin County.* N.p.: Self-published, 1997.

Kappes, William E., and Erwin Petzinger. *The Franklin County Infirmary and Alum Crest Nursing Home, 1832–1984.* N.p.: Self-published, 1984.

Kelton, Dwight H. *Kelton Family Items.* La Mesa, CA: Edwin C. Kelton, 1962.

Lapponi, Giuseppe. *Hypnotism and Spiritism: a Critical and Medical Study.* New York: Longmans, Green & Co., 1907.

Lentz, Ed. *Columbus: The Story of a City.* Charleston, SC: Arcadia Publishing, 2003.

Pollard, James E. *History of the Ohio State University: The Story of Its First Seventy-Five Years, 1873–1948.* Columbus: Ohio State University Press, 1952.

Schlegel, Donald M. *The Columbus Catholic Cemetery: History and Records, 1846–1874.* Columbus, OH: Columbus History Service, 1983.

———. *The Columbus City Graveyards.* Columbus, OH: Columbus History Service, 1985.

Schoyer, George. *History of the Ohio State University Libraries, 1870–1970.* Columbus, OH: Office of Education Services, Ohio State University Libraries, 1970.

Sheridan, Phil. *More about Those Wonderful Old Downtown Theaters.* Columbus, OH: self-published, 1984.

———. *Those Wonderful Old Downtown Theaters.* Columbus, OH: self-published, 1978.

———. *Those Wonderful Old Downtown Theaters, Volume 3.* Columbus, OH: self-published, 1992.

Skipper, James Everett. *The Ohio State University Library, 1873–1913.* Ann Arbor: University of Michigan, 1960.

Smith, Robin. *Columbus Ghosts: Historical Haunts of Ohio's Capital.* Worthington, OH: Emuses Inc., 2002.

Tuttle, Hudson, and James M. Peebles. *The Year-Book of Spiritualism for 1871.* Boston, MA: William White and Company, 1871.

White, Ruth Young. *We Too Built Columbus.* Columbus, OH: Stoneman Press, 1936.

Woodyard, Chris. *Haunted Ohio II: More Ghostly Tales from the Buckeye State.* Beavercreek, OH: Kestrel Publications, 1992.

Wooley, Charles F, and Barbara A. Van Brimmer. *The Second Blessing: Columbus Medicine and Health in the Early Years.* South Egremont, MA: Science International Corporation, 2006.

Periodical Articles

Columbus Evening Dispatch. June 23, 1909.

———. June 24, 1909.

———. March 23, 1913.

———. March 24, 1913.

———. March 25, 1913.

———. March 26, 1913.

Columbus Gazette. July 29, 1824.

Daily Ohio Statesman. November 6, 1851.

———. April 1, 1859.

Hesperian 1, no. 1 (May 1838).

Lentz, Ed. "As It Were: Costume Shop a High Street Highlight." *This Week New Albany.* June 8, 2006.

Muscatine Journal. May 29, 1962.

Ohio State Journal. December 30, 1856.

———. May 6, 1857.

———. April 5, 1859.

———. June 28, 1859.

Ohio Statesman. February 11, 1846.

Plain Dealer. December 24, 1910.

Portsmouth Daily Times. February 5, 1925.

ZIG ZAG (September–October 1998).

Websites

"Dayton VA Medical Center, Ohio." United States Department of Veterans Affairs, http://www.dayton.va.gov/museum/intro.asp.

Kappa Kappa Gamma, http://www.kappakappagamma.org.

About the Author

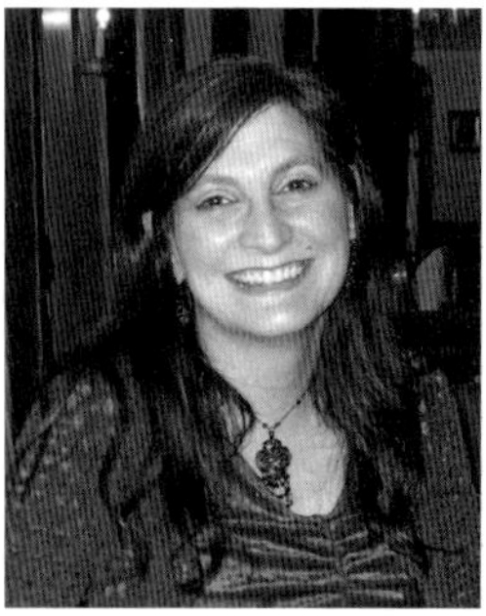

Lifelong central Ohio resident Nellie Kampmann works professionally in the field of history as a museum employee and researcher. She is actively involved with the Kelton House Museum and Garden and the Columbus Landmarks Foundation as a committee member. On the spooky side, her deep interest in the paranormal led her to become a tour guide on the Columbus Landmarks Foundation's yearly ghost tours. She is also a former staff writer for *Haunted Voices Radio*. Nellie lives with her husband, several cats, a dog and a ghost in Columbus.